AZIZA

Barnes, Aziza

ISBN: 978-1-945649-32-5

Edited by Amauta Marston-Firmino
Cover design by Shaun Roberts
Editorial design by Ian DeLucca
Proofread by Rhiannon McGavin

Not a Cult
Los Angeles, CA

Printed in Canada

what had happened was a glitch. ancestral nerve ridden to the point of madness. what had happened— a deer and an armadillo kick it on a Mississippi porch, rain coming down. glitch. there's a you, an I, another name entirely, Two. there's Saint. not who you pray to, but whose offerings allow you to survive. glitch. when you're you, you're in your dad's apartment growing up, his mother sings *La Boheme* on the fire escape, no escape for her. glitch. a comedy store, 2AM peaking, an Afro glistens under club lights, sweat of the father and his father and plantation whole of them. glitch. sankofa, I guess, when I'm an I. tough bird to hit with any number of stones. glitch. English. a language crippled with the lazy poetry of idioms and no feeling. glitch. no windows, casino-like. it's a mental hospital. you didn't lose your mind, you became it. infinitely worse. glitch.

it was so hot there were dead roaches i love you and then
it got roaches you had a lot of last name going on and i
woke up bleeding thru linens a rack of ribs is the style i
bleed out on linens with a messy bitch when i feel ignored
or like staying alive 2 tumblers of champagne and tits out if i
want i wake up with dirt caked lined as in caulking between
skin and nail i can't stay awake without breaking my heart i
break into houses change my name for an interval see how
the other half tastes the first time i felt a chill on my face in
months the white man who lives in my head not far from the
white man who lives in a slave castle and would point from
a balcony down to a blk someone and that day she would
feel water on her body smell like an ocean she couldn't see
for his for him for a crippled arch and rush to the end of the
world took a swig of Jim Beam and a choir of yielded crop
sprung out my chest where the blonde hairs grow a dark·
omen from the nothing-black-about-me comment section i
lose weight in my feet and watch videos of white children
shooting deer for the first time there's no such thing as a
fixed location the deer cocks her head at the child's step to-
ward him loosens the thrill of her name i believe you love
me until i'm sitting in a bar of fluorescent purple and i know
you're thinking of someone you lived with before i fucked
you until somewhere she is a meter high a man in Mississip-
pi sees me when i'm walking in bedstuy i'm just a ghost nig-
gas and he's more sure of my body than i am smoke socket
liquor bound i am my grandfather's cursed extension i am
nothing if not my colonizer's bastard cum i am nothing but
nothing but i am warm and riddled with life occasionally
a deer will walk in front of my porch occasionally albino
lizards crawl into my home and die i know this is my dad
begging a skeleton isn't hard to wait for you just have to
clear your schedule it's tax season and flu season and i don't
say cotton it's offensive and the men sometimes have hands
so big my throat lengthens choke me out and when i pick up
air someone will be left knocking the blonde field

The I is unreliable. Has a birthright with an ugly, clinical name, so let's just skip it.

You are intimated by how much pain a body can hold. Your father sings you to sleep, on the nights he doesn't play Ken Burns's Civil War tapes, the sounds of slaves bellowing "Jacob's Ladder," the recitation of Union and Confederate soliders' letters home. Mosquito bites and ant colonies converge on your fingers, under your bed. He's not a bad man, he's just a man and that is sometimes hate enough. You tell him one day that he's not technically an "African American," because his lineage doesn't go to slave ships, doesn't hail from Ghana and the great con of the millennia, the first slim door of No Return. Your father yells at you, says he's as blk as you are, and even in the diatribe that follows from him, you know you're right and he's less right. He's hidden his iteration of blkness, otherness, in your mother, whose people come from Ohio by way of Virginia by way of a boat from a part of West Africa that remains unsayable because that fascist regime kept poor or no records. When he sings you to sleep, it's a song asking rhetorically, what do you dream? The ants underneath your bed are from the time you ate a Granny Smith apple at night and didn't want to leave your room to go to the kitchen in the dark, just to throw it away. You wake up to a line of black legs and antennae making hill and canyon of you, of your sister. Later in life, around the time you claim your father is another kind of blk, you recognize the presence of insects in your home as a call to the end of days, terrestrially and of your mind, a signal to a certain inheritance, a collection of names to address your brain, now that every canal and neural pathway synapse has chemically gone awry. Your dad says it comes from your mother's side, the African American side, he doesn't specify.

i hear the Rhine Valley is explicit most times of the year since world war what number again the number for again we kept doing it and we is you know who is they is the Againers the Just One More Time cohort of fuckdom and fascism i was 5 when my mom got her first set of all-white couches never exhumed them from their plastic some things are better when suffocated a couch is not one of these things things are not breath-workers i should not be able to be lodged in plastic

my mama has pneumonia today a fever of 103 degrees which was lower than the temperature outside my cousin's graduation in Las Vegas when i was 12 and by then thoroughly molested and worn to the nub of my own hands that failed failed failed they touched the leather interior of my dad's Lexus my two failures connected to my wrists in the same car i once hallucinated 6 spiders growing out of and into each other after my left hand was impaled by a small wooden stick too large to truly be a splinter how my sister and i hated an odd number decided ugly them all but 3 a divinity a church and there were 3 white couches not one of which that neighbor touched me on

God bless the plastic magnitude of the zombie child when my sister almost died of pneumonia at 2 i was jealous *why does she get to die?* her lungs lined and plastered full i was so lonely i almost prayed my molester would stop by just to stare at me until i became still a piece of white embalmed again

The I is fixated, but not endeared to explanation. The I is not attracted, but in a polarity locked onto a few moments in the I's existence. Hi, I.

You are confused entirely by men who dress up, even seasonally appropriately, as Santa Claus. Eating steak in the morning is American, with eggs, American, with Orange Juice or Vodka, American. You are American with a caveat. You get anxious in the middle of days that are considered, even by your own standards, joyful. The current understanding you've acquired is each revelation of selfhood is a door of No Return, is you going from captivity, a jailed uselessness, to a slave of another God. And this is the hope of evolution, going from smelling the imagined ocean to boarding a boat atop it, a journey, however removed from your own command. Then becoming American as Orange Juice. As Santa Claus. As Seasons. The more you know of yourself, the farther you are from anything you've ever understood. You grow slimmer entering each door, leaving the salt-sacked cities you once read your name into, hearing the swift echo, a pronouncement. Often, you are positive, that there are five of you at a card table, dressed in red velvet, competing for the official narrative of your life. Poker is played, bourbon is in glass tumblers had, the soft texture stretching over each body committed to stains and wear. They yell, a bray kin to each auntie and grandmother in the bloodline, only invested purely in cruelty. Their nails talons, barefoot, blk Joan Crawfords, calling you a useless bitch, a hot mess, a too much, a that nigga won't love you, a you'll just fuck it all up, a you fat and it's not cute cuz you got a lil' frame, and the like. You swear it was 10AM just two seconds ago and now it's 138PM and you can't understand it. The five of you scream in your head as you walk in your black socks, the ones with with words, "No Nonsense" stitched into them, into the delicate rain, a water unusual to you. Who owns you now?

5

WHO OWNS YOU NOW?

Parlor, Southern, Plantation style house. The year is tobacco time, when that crop was famous and famous for making white men rich and famous, for new black chattel to tend the fields of it. Even though you were born in LA in 1992, you are here. The crops are high, a blonde field. In the parlor, you sit across Confederate General TJ "Stonewall" Jackson, who is smoking what appears to be a fat blunt. A TV is between you both, Ken Burn's Civil War tape glitching methodically on the drawn image of Stonewall, giving a fiery sermon to his battalion of soldiers. You're manacled to the gilded chair you sit in.

You're 8. And then not. And then, you exist here.

STONEWALL
Is the slave capable of love?

YOU
What's the hypothesis.

STONEWALL
Given the shape of the skull and given the size
of the forehead and given the width of the lips
and given the scope of the nostrils and given
the inconsistency of the ears and given the
radius of the waist on the women and given
the kink of the curl and given the depth of the
palm lines and given the amount of water in
the irises and given the wail in the throat and
given the warble in the throat and given the
soprano in the throat and given the baritone in
the throat and given the grief. In short, no.

YOU
Grief is an appendage now? A body part?

STONEWALL
They way you all walk would suggest it.

YOU
God is something about this.

STONEWALL
To blame? Careful.

YOU
I didn't say that.

But you kinda did. You're remembering the fury of being an I; someone who knows her own name. Owns her own name. Every night you lay down to sleep, you become property to the five women who reside in your head, the lowest rung of chattel, as they also serve Stonewall. They are coming up fast and outward, leaving the chambers of your mind, and expanding into the room you're chained to. This is the part of you Stonewall loves most-- that you can't contain yourself.

The five of you drape yourselves around Stonewall, massaging his shoulders, rolling another blunt at his feet, giving him a manicure, combing his mane, turning the pages of the Bible in his lap. You can't believe you, but this is your burden.

You begin to think of the phrase "this too shall pass" and how it applies to victories. You figure in your waking life, you're having a bout of sleep paralysis.

YOU
Why do you need this. This much of me.

STONEWALL
Not everyone gives themselves up so easily.
Answer me why you do that? How you can,
even? Is this how all slaves are?

YOU
When did you purchase me?

STONEWALL
If you can't remember, that's more telling than
my ownership.

YOU
You're saying I'm practiced.

STONEWALL
I'm saying, you recall how that boy Kenny
in your class accused you of wanting to be a
slave because you cried during that education-
al reenactment video about the black girl who
is taught to write her name in the dirt?

YOU
I recollect.

STONEWALL
Kenny is a smart one.

YOU
Just because I can feel doesn't mean I want to
be bought.

STONEWALL
That you cry in public. That you can't scream
or get angry without breaking out in hives.

That you curve your spine inward to walk lower, looking at your feet when the memory of your white man grandfather would've slapped your head upward.

                    YOU
Sometimes in my head I'm a white man.

                    STONEWALL
Thank God.

                    YOU
For real, I'll have these intricate fantasies where I'm in Royal, Medieval England, wearing the whole get up. The knickers and long socks and coat with the string strapping it up. My hair is high, my beard at shadow, a small, single pearl earring. And I'm dancing with the women at court. A free man, but I don't think about being free because I've never been anything else.

                    STONEWALL
Science fiction.

                    YOU
Power. It's power.

                    STONEWALL
I may have to begin to own you in the day as well as the nights.

YOU

Gotta stop watching these fucking tapes.

STONEWALL

That's your kink, though. Being controlled by
someone you find repulsive. Resisting.

YOU

I-

The five of you freeze and stare into their source. You don't
like it when you lie, when you even make the first syllable
to lie. You give yourself away. What's ingrained in child-
hood, the nerves hardwiring, that's the pocket you reside.
One of you, the one with the Bible, throws the book at you.
It opens to the chapter Ezra, where your name is written.
Couldn't have been the first time it was written in history,
but it's an early incantation. The Precious One. What is
it, to be precious? To prize? The you combing Stonewall's
hair approaches, combs yours. Divides the hair into rows,
cornrows. You are surely 8, beads at the bottoms. You get
the beads from your breast, enclosed in the red dresses
each of the women in your mind who are you wear. You
want not only to become someone else, but something else
entirely. You never miss a funeral, you barely exist even
though you overpopulate a room. A deer crosses the win-
dow in the parlor, your head bobbing with each pull and
weave of the hair atop it. The deer stares at you. What else
can it do? You know one of the ways for a deer to die is
similar to your own; hunted for sport.

STONEWALL

So now you want to be big game, huh?

YOU

What was the last thing you said before you
died?

STONEWALL

Let us cross over the river and rest under the
shade of the trees.

YOU

You wait.

STONEWALL

Old trick. I'm eternal here.

YOU

Ugh. Sick.

STONEWALL

It's in your blood.

YOU

In mine?

STONEWALL

A sickness. A chemical imbalance.

YOU

Same's yours.

STONEWALL

Fervor isn't the same as instability.

YOU

I guess we could call you sane-passing.

STONEWALL
It's already going to be a mess. Once the men
learn they can touch you.

YOU
My mom won't talk to me about that part.

STONEWALL
You're a parasite. So needy. Stand up, as a
man would.
Face me, eye to eye.

YOU
Like a duel?

STONEWALL
At least the end of this.

Stonewall takes out a pistol from his pocket, cleaning it
with a kerchief. He paces backwards 10 steps. The deer
still stares at you. You're good at imitations. You stare
back. You could become her. Slide into the pelt, break
your hands down into hardened hooves. You'd never dance
again, but then you'd never talk again-- the list of never
agains would be long.

YOU
I don't think that's gonna work out for me.

STONEWALL
Try.

You sit in the parlour, until your skin is fur. Your braids
bury into your skull. The 5 other women who are you fol-
low suit. The room is full of 6 deer. Practice. You still be-
long to anyone but yourself, cultivating a liberation ritual.

What will you be when you wake up.

Having hidden in another body, the I has demands. Hidden in a you, hidden in a deer, the I can scream into their own void.

Curve my fingers around the fat in a glass jar. Come up with shine dewy & I am 8, asking what it is— the drops on a succulent at 7am. *It's dew. Stupid.* The fuck I know about water anyway, calling me stupid for. Los Angeles & everyone pronounces it under the more white colonizer, *LAS ANGELIS,* & I curb to the water that won't die.

I do this.

Rub into the rind on top of the bone this oil & I see the
scab from when I shouted, from my bike to his small car,
excuse me sir to a man & he did nothing but drive forward
more & more & unmoved & of course my bike hit the curb
& of course I went flying & forgot how it felt, the flight, if
I enacted it, & of course I didn't enact it & the man, blk &
in this town of whites who pray to a confederate so & so
unnamed but buried well, said *I would have never forgiven
myself if I really hurt you* & I apologize to the man, the blk
man, for my being so in the way of him, so easily a deer.

In headlights, them fools lose the staring contest their ge-
netic makeup evolved them into doing real well: staring.
Never run from the light, but stare into it as if they could
bend the light back like my hair pulled back & neck with
it down & with the lights the car, with the lights the gas,
the lights the gas with it the oil. I do this. Now my breasts,
which piss me off for being there. I am 8 & my mama has
a blue slip this water crisis would convince poor blks is
water, *just wring it out & the drops will come,* call them
dew & me stupid when the shit won't dry into a memory,
dry into something I can say ain't happen. *Put this on,* &
the one instructing me is a girl, is from up the street, is
older & not by much but by enuf that she has a 17-year-old
brother who is always in his room or throwing balls in the
air & over my head like he can't see below certain bones.
Put this on &

I do this,

throw on a silk blue in a closet where there are nails jutting out from the wood, *it's an old house, but a good house,* & there's an excuse for the tetanus an excuse for the infection & none for me, who gets dressed to get undressed in a closet anyway in her mama blue slip no less lest you must be the one for burning wearing the hottest way to incinerate dumb bitch dumb bitch & what could I know about all that, laying on top of her, her saying,

> *you're pretty & my wife, welcome home honey* or *honey I'm home* or *come out honey I'm home* or *honey honey honey honey you dumb bitch of honey you honeycombed stupid you dewy dumb bitch say whatever you want but I'm in your home ha ha I'm in your home ha ha & your mama don't know about me ha ha come out honey I'm home & wearing a suit ha ha don't you know your name honey it's honey honey honey honey I'm home put this on I'm in your home & what what what dumb honey stupid comb bitch your come I'm out in wife welcome blue honey slip bitch ha ha your your your dew don't honey a dumb bitch* & the bitch of it

was that was a good Tuesday afterschool. & I could be 8, but more likely I'm 23 when I do this, rub into a pimpled chest the oil. Coconut which I'm told is good by those who are good by those who are in the morning because they know when to wake up. Jimmy is a name for a white boy & I am aware of white boys. Jimmy is a white boy who walks me home from school. Jimmy is a long nickname for James. James is the name of a white boy who is my grandfather. My grandfather moved into another apartment in the South Bronx when my grandma died & painted all the walls black. My grandfather is named James and never nicknamed into a longer name Jimmy & he drank a fifth of Jim Beam every day & sat in the black apartment he painted without my grandma who was black but not like the wall like a rotting banana or a more just world. Jimmy is a name for white boys & he walks me home. Jimmy is a name for white boys you don't think about having desire even though they discuss sex. Sex is a honey bitch blue slip for me I am considering wearing flag pole distant but I am into my hips okay into a gleam from them so we ain't there yet, state status, country bound & oath. Jimmy is a white boy who walks me home & says I am pretty *you're so pret-ty with your beard & all it was one of the first things I liked about you that you weren't afraid to show the hair on your chin that you just wore it out there I liked that about you about you & that beard I liked that.* Jimmy sits on my porch. Jimmy says *it's cold can we go inside?* Jimmy walks in my bed & takes of his shoes & I know the smell of feet is a commitment & the room is different the room is a dewy bitch the room is honey wife & why is Jimmy, a white boy name my grandfather wouldn't give to himself if he laughed in the black room at my grandma's dead banana peel body in the dew of 7am & I'm 8 &

> *you're pretty & my wife, welcome home honey* or *hon-ey I'm home* or *come out honey I'm home* or *honey honey honey honey honey you dumb bitch of honey you hon-eycombed stupid you dewey dumb bitch say whatever*

you want but I'm in your home ha ha I'm in your home
ha ha & your mama don't know about me ha ha come
out honey I'm home & wearing a suit ha ha don't you
know your name honey it's honey honey honey honey
I'm home put this on I'm in your home & what what
what dumb honey stupid comb bitch your come I'm out
in wife welcome blue honey slip bitch ha ha your your
your dew don't honey a dumb

bitch but Jimmy, a white boy who walks me home in Mississippi in 2016 in the snatch of magnolias crawling out of the air to greet my neck, he isn't a bad man.

He isn't a bad man like I am a bad man

a bad one who flings sex like small rocks out of a sling into
the air around my neck around my neck is the bullet hole in
the Lyceum meant for James Meredith, another James not
Jimmy, another laugh-less government wrung out into dew.
Jimmy kisses my cheek & my lips & the break of my face.
Jimmy crawls on top of me & begins to make a motion, to
make a concession to pump dryly onto my pants.
Jimmy notices I've stopped breathing, become lax as hon-
ey *welcome home honey* & calls me a bitch in so many
words, the words, *look. I'm gonna be nice about all this.
But that? That hurt me.*

That being no.

My no.

Out of my mouth, I swear & still somehow smoke to him.

Inaudible.

How can't he hear me?

I'm still saying it.

What if I'm not even here.

What if I stop trying.

And I stop.

The no out my mouth & never mind I said though my jaw
was dew & lax & only would appear in the morning. Never
mind the thank God I didn't wait until morning with a Jim-
my not James in my bed wet & scrambling

*this could work why won't you let it work why can't you
enjoy me a good thing I am a good man named Jimmy
you are a bitch I will be nice about welcome home you
honey fuck let me fuck you I said you were pretty &* sure-
ly I am 8 & yo, we

ain't been properly introduced,

*my name is the precious one. My dad picked it out in
'76. It's in the bible in Ezra. I'm a minor character. &
I do this. Rub into my body the villain to water. It slides
off me. Not even the dew can ride my back.*

I stand in the rain & that's where I meet you.

By now, the kneecaps are prize onions. The breasts are at-
tractive in that dumpling manner. The stomach is simply
greased & arrogant. The thighs. Here we are at the hair.
Oil natty in the hair. Insufferable this ugly weight of brown
catching dirt & Jimmy didn't walk home after I asked him
to leave. That's why I coat the thighs in oil. He came back.
Opened the back door to my room & said

*please don't be mad at me. I'd hate it if you were mad at me
& you're on the phone like I thought you would be. Mad at
me. Please don't. Pretty honey wife dumb suit comb ha ha
don't be mad slip don't be blue mad don't be me hate wife
would let's talk about all this.*

I am dew & shine. I am kind & deer stare. I am the car
bending into a blue slip of no more name. *Can I have a ride
home?* I give to you a ride home. I give to you a consola-
tion. I don't touch you & you say nothing, even though you
told me you're being *nice about all this.* Who was I going
to tell? The oil. On my body.

I like this.

This?
Sitting here with you. Pretending you're mine.
It could be bloodless. One dog. One man-person. One
house. I point to the furniture in Saint's house: [The
leather sofa]
Does this one have a story?
No.
[The stereo system]

This?

Nah.

[A cluster of framed photographs, no clearly visible face
among them]
These?

Yea. They do.

Okay. This?

We map out the furniture that is ahistorical from the fur-
niture that is riddled with The Woman of The House. I
want her name. I want to take her driver's license and
skin, her mother's waist memory of her inside and lurch
outward, I want to become her and to have always been
her so I can have this house, this
Saint, this dog, this furniture speckled with memory of
me and not, diseased with mine mine mine and not. I'd
be a white woman with a good tan. In love and hard to
kill.

I keep drinking Saint's red wine that he keeps in the fridge even though I know you're not meant to do that to red wine, chill the body and the glass. I hold his hand in my hand. The blonde hairs on my wrist and shoulders run up like wheat incapable in a gust. His freckles like my grandfather's freckles. His eyes, my grandfather's eyes. In a way, I hate him— Saint playing house as a white man, leaving his black body outside, as I do my black body.

I'd love you and our dog.

This isn't my dog.

It's our dog tonight.

What are we naming her?

Saint and I play house. We float on the stratosphere of this relationship. We buoy on the air above this house and point to what we own.

Let's name her Charleston.

I'd walk around barefoot and dance every day you came home.

You already do that. If we stay these people, you'd never have to celebrate me coming home.

A week before, I listened to a Gladys Knight song about this *if I were your* and I refuse to feel sick about it. This is a tax. A war tax. I'm allowed to become her. He's allowed to become him. We're allowed to fall in love for one night with the ones that get to come home alive.

Honey, how was your day? Baby, they don't want me.
At the office? Did you talk to Charlie about a raise?
Saint, they want to kill me.
Don't ruin this. Not this. I'm hungry.
Your dinner is in the oven. I knew you'd be home late.

I keep making new routes home. The police know all them anyway. Them?
Us.
What did you cook for me? This.

I play *It's Been Such A Long Time.* The album cover is a blk woman in a giant feather headdress, diamonds, bikini. She is cracking out of an egg. The egg is black.

Dance with me, baby. Arms first?
Waist first.

When we dance, the dog whose name is Bird keeps running to play with Saint and Saint has to keep throwing a toy to get the dog to go in the dinning room and the dog named Bird keeps running back to our feet which are preoccupied with lifting and falling and lifting and falling into the rug that has no memory with this white folk's home. Sardis Lake would be our spot; Saint, teaching me how to noodle for catfish. Saint, teaching me how to suck clean poison from a snake bite at his ankle.

Saint, rubbing my feet, his knees in a sand dune, looking up at me and the sun behind my head, refusing to close his eyes, so blue the sun deliberates with him a shutter. The dog named Bird, always an addition to our calves, needing to be needed, needing a task simple as catching a light roundness and running it back to the source of its flight.

I'm not allowed to love Saint like this. I rent him. He rents me. We pretend. We try each other on for size. I crook my head into the dew basin of his collar. I cry in front of him and laugh like I'm painting his walls the color of my breath. I look like my grandmother, for a moment, then not. Saint looks like my grandfather James. Even if he were mine.

Even if I could bear a kid out of me, of him. I'd be saving no one. I'd bear another I. The I would lose their names in a bar. Lose their names in a chamber. Lose their names in a classroom under the nail and callous of an English teacher in a semester's worth of epithet. If Saint is a dress, the zipper is flesh hungry. I take him off.

You know I would love you. I'd cook salmon with white wine sauce and order the New York Times for you.
I thought you didn't like men that way. I don't.

And Saint is alight. A choice is in the center of his rug that has no memory. And I don't want him to pick me up. I don't want to become a body responsible, charged with blood and its consequence. I just wanted to rent a white man and be a white woman and a life I didn't inherit. I don't want to suffer because I had to try her man on, because my name got lost, because I wanted to die over a word and another word that wasn't my name. I am a quiet unravel in the dark and I still don't believe I am here *are you here* and Saint alone

can answer and if Saint touches me now, in this room, this room for guests, if he crosses the rug without a name just as I don't got one after tonight and the almost wasting in a dive bar for hicks and pathetics, if he does, I break a white woman and the white man I carry in my skin, my grandfather James, my land that's my land. Don't touch me, Saint. And he doesn't. Wouldn't. Loves me good and stays on his side of the room, in a borrowed body.

I cackle like I have an address.

It's hard to stay in I. Unstable. Glitch.

& what is it with all these men there's a distinction between fixation and attraction what you are attracted to is not what you're fixated by your obsession to make stable a fissure in your childhood versus your power a quality evoking interest something was stunted you remember being 8 & seeing her her arms pulled warrior outward her back ridges out pouring short locks cocked clean backward lips & all there wasn't anyone else in the room somehow an empty terrain like the deserts in westerns you are most yourself in front of her most in your body alive she was all you want & still want never forgot that an honest feeling the charge up & thru you how with men there was & is a blanket nothing a push clean into desire a well you guess we're both here a lack of bravery a lack of

there are days where you wonder if you collect men the
way some folks collect coins or dead butterflies in frames
just to say you conquered just to say you could just to be
the man & make them your bitch just to be bigger than
your dad

they're all Saint stone-bodied prehistoric you are hard on
yourself & them on you why won't you do enough get titty
enough kitchen apron & listen to your wounds enough the
5 women in red who are all you scream constantly wax
your pussy paint your nails rebraid your hair coconut oil
every scrap of real estate it's kin to what she yelled at you
when you were 8 & had found your mother's blue slip

you become you become she is now a deer with a blue
pelt headlight accommodating arms now legs now numb to
saving herself she doesn't like she is closer to they a body
of many bodies many routes outward the most theyself
they be the more there is to vomit up a somatic response
to being 8 to being in literal closets a slave in some way to
attraction a slave in other ways to violence

& you guess in a way it was simple. typical. an ancestral flashback, a glitch if we are in fact in the matrix, putting you next to another nameless you on the Clotilde, sweat-wrecked & sullied, it's chemical, a reaction to stimuli, what can you do, a screaming nerve, a jump cut back to Olympia, rock forward to a naked white woman with a black velvet string around her neck, an offering of a bundle of flowers, your face sudden & reductive in the background, you the background again, your hands the only currency against the white paper swaddling the flowers, the only place you're an I is in giving, she gives, they gives, you are in context, a consciousness overwhelmed, you are only somehow an adult an American blk is told a few parables they whole life: Emmett (no one has agreed on a consensus spelling), some version of Jesus & if you're lucky a Black Panther psalm.

in Oxford, Mississippi there are two Confederate statues, one when you first drive into the town, the other when you go down the street onto campus. you salute both. a performance art unto yourself. you are bitter & done & undone. every tree my mama's hair, wind-whipped & round.

you loved her & love her. yes my mama, but now you're talking another woman. white woman. it's funny, white women. & we were at this bar, sitting, ordering, waiting for a drink.

& this guy, a white guy, it's funny, white guys, comes up
to her.
& I guess he calls me what white good ole boys from Holly
Springs call me & calls her what good ole boys from Holly
Springs call her & she comes back to me.

with these words.

& like, they're just words.

Don't die over no damn words, & the fucked up thing is that's all I would die for, made a pact with myself, stood in the rain covered in coconut oil & a glass of box wine about it, after my mama confessed she near died in a train explosion outside D.C. a week prior.

I wanted to tell my ma what I had originally thought that morning, brushing my teeth in the bathroom with the big mirror I often contemplate a last sincere fuck with a man in front of, looking at myself & saying on a loop, *it's over, it's over,* that I wished brushing your teeth was an institution white folk made up to keep they house Negroes in the house a few minutes longer after fucking or rape, if it weren't consensual.

But nah. That shit just good for your teeth. & I can imagine the cackle in her electric Chevy Volt toward Santa Ana on her morning commute, but I ain't say anything about no slave pondering cuz it wasn't that kind of 9am & it wasn't that kind of Friday.

Hungover on brut & good pussy my 5am stroll to my Toyota Corolla on the square is a treat reserved for blk queer bitches the country over, I've decided, hearing the birds, whatever kind, doing they thing as day competes with night for airtime.

This was before my mama call, before the train tracks in D.C. caught fire a second time that month, before my sister explained to me the fights overheard since ma's return to LA, fights with my dad, over they living will & its needed renewal & I guess it does all lead back to some kind of ownership, some kinda blk worried that the name they claim will loose hold on they land. A 40-acre flash back. A big memory PTSD.

It was after I read *The Autobiography of an Ex-Colored Man,* in City Grocery while hearing a table of white women & one gay white man posing as interlocutor signify

> *a large black guy named Nate,*
> who didn't know how to act at their mutual (read, white) friend's wedding

(I believe cutlery & a question of manners was involved).

& it was just

> *something we couldn't teach Nate, you know?*
> *He's so old! You can't teach that kinda thing to all of them.*
> *I just don't think they do manners, but he danced great at*
> *the party. All that sweat on his back!*

> It was most certainly after my 6AM walk to my office, eclipsing the confederate memorial statue behind the buckshot meant for James Meredith's forehead, the statue, a solider ambiguous & atop it, erected in 1907, saluting what?

It was decidedly after I'd been to Water Valley in the company of a 50-some-odd-year-old white woman from Memphis who locked the door of her car faster than I could suggest leaving the property, a subdivision of the land where folk drew up a steel poster that read,

> *JESUS IS COMING GET RIGHT OR GET LEFT.*

Trump they new Christ, irreligious as a New Yorker can get & still make Dixie votes.
Driving with Donna Diggs, whose experience of cruelty enacted itself on her face; her chihuahua mix, in old age &

depravity ate off entirely her nose, the pain an indictment of the word "dizzy," nothing that engaged with cartilage & a question of bone should sound in the family of the word "honey" or any word that leaves your tongue ignorant of blood. I asked her why the white men of the backwood in Water Valley, land-chained cousins to the vultures above our heads, why they were burning their trees.

Because it's their trees,

said Donna & it was most certainly after Donna's reconstructive surgery & our field trip to the charcoal tree stumps that I decided I would die over some words,

perhaps exclusively over some words & it was also after

that white girl in Proud Larry's cozied up to me on Halloween Pride Night, everyone in the bar queer or looking for a story to tell their straight ilk the Sunday morning at Big Bad Breakfast what they done did, what had happened & the was. It was certainly after I asked this white girl, who reads Faulkner & Weatly & is, knowingly or otherwise, a Negrophile,

where did you get that dress?

A WWII pin up uniform & she replied,   *a boutiq ue in*

LA
run by
Latina
s.
They
are
genius
es
with
pin up
gear,

& I say I'd want some for myself, my own body, to wear alone when femininity asks of me a moment to bend, when my breasts don't igg me out & my ass ain't just an interruption to my back, & she responds as if I want these clothes to tease her, always for her, her white body I've never known & will never know, know meaning touch, touch meaning have, & I an intentional have-not, touch-not, know-nothing ass bitch, she says,

& I say

    oh. I just couldn't handle you in something like that, you ain't need to handle shit,

& she admits, drink fully imbibed & digesting, I'm her queer blk fantasy, that if she was down it would go down & I'm steady scanning for the nearest auction block;

where would you like me, missus? How should I stand?

& it was absolutely before this white girl Melissa from Memphis lied to whole scores of miscellaneous muthafuckers that we done fucked & been fuckin' & lied to whole scores of muthafuckers that Gina proposed to her, gave her a ring & everything, when heretofore Gina ain't even gave her a Lifesaver candy or the time of day. It was both before & after a white woman I've never touched decided my body was her business.

Everyone white wants a collar around your neck, wants to take you on walks & tell other whites your name.

> It's perpetual like that, fast & slow as the lifespan
> of a rottweiler, & when you run away
> they'll say you bit them
> & hunt.

But it was also before one particular white woman said to me,

I want you,

& could tell me my true middle names & what I ate for breakfast that morning & I said it back,
I want you,

& did, mouth open wanting more than my 4 names could pronounce but never having, never owning, never throwing a stick in the mud & claiming mine hers, hers mine, no, the way we became was more sitting on a porch swing until you assume your body was also made of wood, also made of chain & wind to push thru, that you ain't even the sum of your parts, ain't even parts, just the wind thru a chain, thru a fat wet of pine exhaling the memory of a tree. I would cling to her, even in the echo of a man in Queens, New York, who insisted I didn't love him the way he loved me, & I would lie, not even knowing it a lie,

> *you're wrong baby, I love you just the*
> *same, just equal, just enuf,*

because I thought it made more sense, to love the swollen back of a man black & rich with lips, thighs & broken from white eyes upon that same back. I thought it made more sense to dream up a life with him, a kitchen counter & all its sin atop me, me atop him. I thought it added up quicker & to a higher number, waiting for him, waiting for New York again, the blood & bandage of that place, where I knew most corners, where I could yell in the street at white supremacy & be safely ignored.

It was surely after I met his mother in Florida & accidentally made her weep over the sauce for her jerk chicken when I asked her if she ever owned a pet & she screamed before encasing her mouth with her hand, no wedding band saddling it,

oh God! & I felt that

the mango tree in the back should have grown sentient enuf to hurl me into a field of wayward ducks with a branch, she told me one dog from her childhood burned to death in a sugarcane field fire,

the children, those bad children, chased him into it & that

& that was it & the second, with her husband, she suspected murdered the dog, by gun or negligence & that, that was it for dogs & I didn't speak for a clean 15 minutes, which is long in a house you've never been to before, in a state you'd only seen the inside of the airport, with a man you'd only met 5 months before, who said he loved you before he knew all your names, when he assumed the one you give everyone is the one your parents had the doctors write down on your birth certificate.

& it was after, of course, after after after, I watch white truckers park their trucks, walk out with Marlborough golds & original flavor Redbulls, sipping on the divider with black men whose sweat encircles the space under their shoulders, a full wet shape & the bugs are dead, organs splayed on my windshield which I've often thought of as purely a deterrent for wind & people until 80 mph became a speed I knew intimately, then yea. In Mississippi, on highway W 278, that shield just for the bugs. The blk woman I'm on the phone with in this sudden parking lot in this sudden woods & parade of restless truckers, she so beautiful it's stupid & I feel stupid hearing her voice, knotted in my collarbone, her laugh & all my other damn plans getting canceled. For an hour on W 278, two blk queer women could fall in some iteration of love while the steeples to the left & right of my car did not become knives, that the white truckers, carriers of unknown cargo, were swatting flies & not the smell of me. My particular lust.

It was after I struck below E in my car & hyperventilated when the GPS satellite was out of sync telling me I was actually nowhere & finally felt it. Nowhere. Nowhere, 38655. Nowhere, USA. A place I always knew I had a zip code in, now baring its back to me, full & unfortunately alive in Nowhere with my dad on the other end of the phone saying,

> *you don't see a street light? A gas station? A sign for a gas station?*

& I know he means a human-made light, a manufacture of safety & no, I didn't but if I did, which human made it, but if I did, would it be safer than living in Nowhere? I thought about posting up then, gas-less, void of option & having the longest night of my life, on the border of Nowhere & Nowhere Else, which is between highway 5 & 278, if you're considering a visit.

That blk woman didn't love me & don't now but I don't
have to be good to be tolerated, I don't have to have a good
big love to avoid being killed. I can be flippant & thrown.
She can hurt & throw me. I met the partner I knew she had
in Detroit & her hand felt like a fisherman's nightmare, all
the catch preemptively dead in the sea. & she's allowed to
live, too.

    & it was around the time my mama told me

        she nearly exploded with the train in DC during
        that electrical explosion, but by now it's hard to
        recall what happened first,
        the day I decided I would die over some words or
        the day my mama damn near died,

        all the words that I didn't allow to kill me taking
        instead
        my grasp on what happened first.

Around then, my mama voice clean off my ear, I have
to teach a room full of Ole Miss undergraduate students,
most white, a handful blk, & isn't that biblical, a handful,
a handful of bodies, a handful of blood full body & small-
er than the greater portion of you, also in want, always a
handful where the hand is 3 fingers instead of a full five.

& I am crying & admit it to them,

    yes I am crying, no I don't want to talk about it,

& I guess it was the honesty that compelled it, compelled
my student Zach, a white boy in the back of the class to
come up to me afterward & ask
    do you want some drugs?

& I say   *absolutely not thank you.*

& he says   *I wasn't trying to presume* & I say

       I know & no, thank you & I say it so fast I have no

humor quick bite because I fear the feds want my name because I fear white men & their offerings of comfort &

I ask for a kiss on my nose the night before from a man who is white the way my grandfather I do not know is white his eyes a reason to break back toward new religion or burn on a pyre for your country & sanctified pussy, & he does, David does, soft & spilling onto the basin of my upper lip, so close to what he won't do, kiss me, in full, so close I know God will have a lesson for me sunlight or bird clap &

she is unfurling beneath me over me when a woman takes in my breath a small me, 8 & wanting to die out of her neighbor's bathroom window, screams

                thank you
& invokes the same one I pray to, temple my incense an offering what my rented form is & my student Zach, who isn't worried about his grade, but is worried about Jay Z & Beyoncè's relationship

& my eyes rough red & barking never seen a blk bitch un-governed, I suppose

& normally I never say normal but I don't cry outside my house when not in New York & all he can offer my face, my family on the other end of my heart, is
                  some drugs

not even specifying the type or worth or discount I would surely get, just

some drugs

& isn't that me, dammit, the cry I cry of

some   always wanting   *some*

bothered & cooled to untouch Zach unfortunately has seen me with a head wrap on this afternoon in class & honestly, I forgot his name until he reminded me of it. I don't think about you Zach & I don't want any part of your offering of ways out in my head are 5 bad bitches who won't let me rest & one is my mother who this morning called to say she was in a train explosion, electrical on the tracks in DC unkept & her first thought

        as all the families screamed,

        as all the men crawled the windows like pathetic
        ants void of Queen or acid, my mama tells me she
        heard in her head the anger

        of my sister my father at her being killed so quickly,
        she couldn't give them a call.

I walk into the rain barefoot, water collecting high in my red wine a glass made of birds & I salve my body in oil to argue with nature & unblend & I shower first, rub from grapefruit squeezed from my family's tree in Los Angeles, avoiding my eyes red hatch unfurled, & lavender & dirt because this is the way we embalm when our mamas almost die.

When our mamas almost die, confederate statues still have human Klansmen to sit underneath them on Sunday afternoons. I buy a plate of grits & cornbread & watch them,

the Sunday after my mama almost died, before the night I
decided I would die over someone else's words. Figured it
my ancestral right, a right to watch the men who want to
kill me not kill me. I drink a liter of champagne, I get drunk
as my grandfather, white enuf to be the Klan's new Jesus,
surely would & did, his 1/5th of Jim Beam a day proper use
of early formaldehyde.

> I nodded my head at one of them, them Confeder-
> ate flag supporter I happened upon. He was on his
> Harley.

> He nodded back. He revved his engine so loud I
> jumped. Then they all did. Then they left.
> A small chorus of smoke, revving left to highway 7,
> Tupelo & Memphis & Holly Springs.

My grandfather's voice in my head screaming *don't walk
with your eyes on your feet.*

I hear the name Holly Springs & I'm thankful I feel em-
balmed. & there ain't many other places for me to hide.
The words I planned to die over that weren't mine, the
white women taken into account, the mama undead &
back West, my students seen & taken out of the retelling
as suspects, the white woman I love & am allowed to stay
alive with, the white man I love who kissed the basin of my
mouth, the white man who is my grandfather who walks
behind me 3 paces, drinks brown & marries browner, who
I will never resemble save for the blonde hairs crawling out
of my shoulder blades that no white recognizes as a form
of kinship.

> Since all that been laid out.

> It was May. Night. A Mississippi classic.

For blks who date white women to walk in:
a national coffin.

We were at the blind pig, one of the 10 bars on the town square. Oxford looks like a caged paradise for magnolias & white women to appear virginal & blk men to appear toothless. The trees are all my mama's hair, picked out big like she did in the 70's, natty halos no one wants to touch.

you know you love her loved her love her still she was white is white that doesn't change & she is still animated in this body her body which you made yours a possession there was one night where you played dress up with her tried on her lingerie a red lace dress she wore once for you in a photo she praises you so beautiful & you look at yourself believing it you're on her bed eating her pussy this is you your sex your body man & woman & more her moaning you're alive finally alive you almost can't stand the electric you lay together & she talks about excrement her thesis on what leaves the body essentially poop & you laugh make a joke of it the way most men likely would kiss her nipples she chides you take her seriously listen she's white & you've forgotten that in the cleft & dew of her or maybe you remember it fully & integrate it into your consciousness she's white & not like you so you get to be you get to be the blackest person in the room you love her & she sees you she's not trying to excavate you & fill your emptiness with herself your father is not in this room only you are can you maintain this level of joy this amount of presence or will you hide in the false breaks of your childhood self you know the answer even before you ask yourself the question

*You know, I say the word nigger, I say the word dyke; I do!
It's where I'm from I guess & I'm sorry about that, saying
hurtful things but shit that's who I am who I was raised like
& I know what I am but I wouldn't have said it knowing you
both were here. I just wouldn't have done that but see that's
my best friend & I know he's a racist. I know he hates gay
people I know that. & this happens a lot when we go out &
I just have to make sure we get on home because it's that
time. But look okay see okay he lost his son, okay?*

I watch him wait for me to give him a pass.

He lost his son, okay?

How?

He lost him 9 maybe 11 months ago.

No. How did he lose him?

He was 9 years old.

How ain't how old he was.

He got hit in the head with a baseball in the diamond.

Okay.
& he lost him. He ain't been the same, he really hasn't.

Okay.

*& he drinks too much. He just misses his son. He doesn't
know why he's gone.*

Okay.

He was just a kid.

Okay.

They were just playing ball. A Sunday you know?

Okay.

That's why he called you a nigger dyke, you two dykes.

Okay.

He was just sad about his son.

Okay.

He misses him; do you understand? He's in pain.

Somebody wrote *the slave is incapable of love.* Did I understand a parent not know why their son was taken from them? What harm that could do, what you could do walking around with a harm like that? Jeremy from Holly Springs asks me in the blind pig about a white dude who hates any love that ain't his now that one love from him was taken. About a son being there & then not being there in the span of hours, after 9 months of getting here & years of staying here just for the sake of becoming? Did I understand that, the white man from Holly Springs asks me, could I fathom such an occurrence? Taken by an errant baseball. What other errant quantitates could I understand? What other rouge agents would I be able to infer an fatal insistence? Does Jeremy mean to ask am I able to understand? *Is the slave capable of love?* Does loss cognate for me? Is he asking have I been to a funeral? Is he asking have I been to a funeral of a dead son? Is he asking have I been to a funeral of a dead son by way of unnatural causes? Is he asking me about the unnatural cause & the force of its effect on humans, which I must not be? Is he asking me to remember that he is a potential unnatural cause? Inexplicable as a baseball hurtling thru a field, a white clot suddenly murderous & intent on the seizure of beauty. Is he asking me to resurrect a ghost, the haint that covers my ma's hands & our home, the one that heard the state I chose to live & brought up the black boy come up dead from a river, the name no black home can withdraw as warning, a name that will not echo any breath in peace. Is he demanding I remember the photograph, a waterlogged boy in a casket, dressed awkwardly in a suit that could not fit a body unmade such as his.

what
th
ey
di
d
d
o

th
ey
al
re
ad
y
d
o
ne
di
d
al
l
I'
m
tri
ne
sa
y.

take the scenic route to heaven without letting anything die
how

good it is   assumes it's good at all
& God at all & God

is what   all the time & he
placed   his hand on the wher-
ever   & said "it is good"
& constructed the finite

& it is

good. { &

} said it is good   due to   the planned

         obsolescence I know you will die so it is good
& if it's hot it's good & if it's worship it's good
& God is involved in that   & verb is involved in
that, a movement   to know your name by,
as in   "he is such a good
man,"
he did something or at least thought about doing something
                                   and so even the
thought,   which is not a hand
reached out,   is still good, all the
time & all the time is. & when   it began it began
unrequited, a loss of what cancels out the noise,
                                   the whole of existence
a tantrum & good   because then consist-
ent it is,   a pattern it
becomes, a reflection until   expansion city
toward the end, every end   with a curse to rip   thru crea-
tion, & we get big, we change   shape, we discolor,
he & I, the we, the God of this,
who already done made this, this all, & named it
& whatever.   existential rimshots & the sun
is small   on the star scale,   so what can
that say   about how we love?   powerful &
small & then.

in the place with no windows there is Saint he lines his mini plastic water bottles across the perimeter of his room basketball on the television old games grey sweats eats a greek salad daily he's in a drop top Mustang on Crenshaw at 1am speeding the air charging against his face he hasn't been outside in 2 years what he wants is so simple the white plastic band around his wrist involuntary shoes and no laces the most creative he's been given credit for being is in here the pay phone rings he's someone's son and you stare he's a hood nigga a boy from your block the block down the street anyway you could've met him anywhere but you met him here twice voluntary then involuntary he doesn't understand you got out then you came back the nurses are bored but one has heard your name before it was processed into the system you know there's no alcohol here but you raid the refrigerator come up oranges and feed compulsively it is all you eat Saint doesn't understand you but that's not the point of being here the nurses check your rooms every 30 minutes after dispensing at random remuron the little yellow pills with the tear drop on the back you're bloodied by John Ham in a back alley you wake up to a nurse just popping her head in you're outside 30 minutes a day you don't and can't touch each other would holding Saint be like holding the brother you don't talk to do you not talk to him because he has an older version of your face and you don't like giving up the surprise or that for 20 years he didn't exist or that you're your father's 2nd child a demotion from the beginning you thought you represented Saint doesn't talk about his father just his mother who keeps putting him in here he says two more bottles to line up today he was a solider meticulous he was a pro wrestler discerning he was a banger a bravery a use me a conduit his eyes are very far apart and he still strolls around like he's actually just at the club it's too late at night to make anything happen but he wants to take in the night air which you learn is drastically different from day air something you knew as a child and gave up knowing as an adult the important things they still give you mirrors but not windows and you don't know if they don't want to see yourself hazily reflected or if they don't want anyone to see you though you are 10 stories up apparently Kanye West is in the room over section B some commotion might lead to leniency another 15 minutes outside it doesn't your hair is an inch high off your head your eyes are too wide and close together your ears are taller than they've been in your life Saint's back is rocks a bag of them curled and curling over you think of other establishments that have no windows prisons slave castles it doesn't take you long to get to slave castles when you left that fake gold earring its shape the outline of Africa underneath a rock at Elmina who were you giving that too was it so important that you give even if to no one you fixate did someone clean it up your offering as refuse did someone find it and wear it and is still wearing it now and on all important occasions is it molding underneath the wet moss of the stone is it ash now was there a smell as it shifted your beard keeps growing and everyone in this place with no windows can't gauge your gender you are a slave to something and that's why you're here Saint too the fact that you're both black is an ancestral charge if you could touch each other you could tap into an alternate reality where you both are driving Mustangs down Crenshaw at 1am but you can't and there's nowhere here to do the things you can't do

IF YOU COULD TOUCH EACH OTHER YOU COULD TAP INTO AN ALTERNATE REALITY

                    SAINT
Not like sexually right?

                    YOU
Nah, just like E.T.

                    SAINT
Or that Sistine Chapel joint?

                    YOU
Yea like God and Adam--

                    SAINT
Connection and whatever.

                    YOU
Exactly.

                    SAINT
              And what you think is finna happen?

                    YOU
Some Octavia Butler shit.

                    SAINT
I think you're having a stroke.

                    YOU
Nah feel me-- the other morning I woke up and
walked out onto my front porch. Saw a small
skeleton on my doormat, being eaten fully by
a swarm of ants. I looked up and saw 4 more
of what became a skeleton-- they were white

lizards. So white they were almost pink. Blue
eyes. I asked around the housing complex,
no one else had this kind of infestation. They
didn't seem to have a native habitat, a home
they actually belonged to. Feel like if I touched
one of them, somehow, it would've been the
end of me. In a way, just looking at them was.

SAINT

So I'm a lizard?

YOU

You're everything that too-white lizard is not.
You're part of me. Not in a way that I love you
or that you love me or that we even have blood
kin close to our main line. We have an older
blood. And we the only two of us that look like
each other in here.

SAINT

I don't look like you.

YOU

I know--

SAINT

You don't.

You peel an orange. The juice stings your cuticles. The
nurse comes up and tells Saint to take his medicine. You're
both getting pale, even though you're both black, and
different shades of black therein. You were lying before.
You're not the only two black people in here. There's an-
other one who just got admitted, who screams in his room
every time he has to try and eat something, which speaks
to the attempt, the way he tried to leave this planet. People

have to be, on a level, creative to be here. The sting in your cuticle is pleasure, somehow. Since being in here requires a straight edge lifestyle and no sex and no touch, you're finding new ways to feel. They don't let you shave, so your beard is longer than Saint's, you have to just be yourself, no passing for full femme here. Here. You are here. That sentence used to be a comfort, is tattooed on a friend's arm, the reminder that you are not out of your body, out of your mind, off the beaten Earth, but that you are here, the temporal shorthand for sanity. But you are here can also refer to simply a location, your mind having very little to do with it. You are here. And so it is. And all other platitudes for not dead yet. You feel as though you've been floating outside your body, hovering just above it, for the better part of 6 months. Your current psychiatrist is a white woman, and full of white feminism, so she doesn't listen to a word you say-- about your pills. All of the ones you've tried. How they give you night terrors. How you can't sleep. How sleep is crucial to mental health. She looks at you like you are the infestation. You are.

                    YOU
        Fine. I don't look like you.

                    SAINT
        Welcome.

                    YOU
        But I'm just saying--

                    SAINT
        Just saying is stupid.

                    YOU
        Why come that is?

SAINT

Cuz it makes it sound like whatever you about
to say shouldn't have that much of an impact.
Like I shouldn't really care, I should just let
you talk. It's not fair, it's rude and fucking own
what's about to come out your mouth and into
my ear. Be more careful. Care more.

YOU

How long since you been outside?

SAINT

2 years.

YOU

Fuck.

SAINT

Uh huh.

YOU

They can do that?

SAINT

You ain't supposed to ask me about that. How
I got here.

YOU

I'm not.

SAINT

You are.

YOU

And you won't tell me?

SAINT
My mom keeps putting me in here.

YOU
Why?

SAINT
Why you keep being in here? You got out
last week, now you're back. The fuck is that
about?

Saint is right. You really shouldn't tell him why or how
you're back in here. It's better, this anonymity, the blank
page in between sections of your life. You struggle with
that in your outside world-- what to tell who and how and
when, the details, the collection of events that make you
you, what's privileged, if anything, are you just spilling
outward. You told him about the white lizards in Missis-
sippi. You thought he'd understand but you don't even un-
derstand it, not really. Once every few weeks, you'd see a
deer outside your door, too. It would stare at you in that
deer way, so long, as if everything else had already gone to
shit except you, loving, in a way. Then it would jump off,
lithe, airborne. You'd worry it would leap into on coming
traffic, seeing as you lived off highway 7 and they have a
tendency to run head on into their doom. If it happened, it
happened when you were gone. You imagined yourself that
deer-- more suited to the environment. You fancied your-
self a nature bitch. You were wrong, and technically it's
okay to not know yourself all the time, but it does have its
disadvantages. You were dying in that mutherfucker, could
swear you could feel blood dripping off the leaves, like
those songs. You stopped being able to trust what was in
front of you, took more pictures of pedestrian things to re-
fer to as truth later-- see the white lizards. They felt like the
manifestation of the devil, alive and crawling through your

house. You grew to believe in demons, real and walking toward you. Really, you have and had your traumas and they were running you ragged. The woman you loved you chased toward you and away. You couldn't let someone you loved see you like this-- unshowered, teeth uncleaned, mind unkempt. But then you wouldn't see her. You weren't used to someone just loving you-- the imperfect, heinous you. The love you remember being comfortable with, understanding, was if you were good-- a notion of perfect, meaning, accessible, functional, pleasing and people pleasing. A servant, in some regards.

She didn't love you that way. She was a big, good love. White, but not like the lizards.

And

you pushed her away. You were very adept at pushing away the good, at that time in particular.

YOU

Outside time.

SAINT

30 minutes.

YOU

After you.

SAINT

Why you can't let me be a man and do man shit?

YOU

Huh?

SAINT

Like hold open the door for you?

                        YOU

I just got here first--

                        SAINT

Whatever.

You're both outside, or as outside as you can be. There's
glass covering the whole of the patio, tall-tall windows,
but they're not opaque like the ones inside. You can see.
Traffic. Chick-fil-A. UCLA students on Bird scooters. It's
Friday night, you remember. You hate this side of LA. But
seeing the traffic now has never been more of a salve. A
true medicine.

                        YOU

It's like-- it's right there.

                        SAINT

Yea.

                        YOU

Smells different.

                        SAINT

Rained earlier, I guess.

                        YOU

You know how much longer they keeping you?

                        SAINT

Don't matter what they say to me.

                        YOU

Not even the doctors?

SAINT
They just observe. And they tell me all kinds
of whatever. Don't matter until I have all my
shit packed and the doors open. Then the next
set of doors. Then the next. Till I'm in the
parking lot. Then in the car. Then down the
405. Then open the door to my house. Then
close the door to my room. Then I'll know
when I'm getting out.

YOU
Fair.

SAINT
You get a lot of calls.

YOU
I know.

SAINT
And you're still that sad.

YOU
I'm sick.

SAINT
We all sick. I'm talking about sad.

YOU
That's a part of this sick.

SAINT
You ain't hearing me.

YOU
And you not listening to me neither.

SAINT

So okay-- if we do the E.T. Thing--

YOU

Like I been saying--

SAINT

What happens?

YOU

We get to-- I dunno. Where do you want to be
right now? Exactly where?

SAINT

In a droptop Mustang. On the 405 at 1am. Air
on my face, air so fast it's finally wind. And
I'm driving, like that, for as long as I want.
The gas don't go out, the oil don't need chang-
ing, I just go. I go until I want to stop.

YOU

Boom. That would happen then.

SAINT

You some kinda woo woo--

YOU

Some kind. Mostly I can't see past where I got
hurt.

SAINT

Where'd you get hurt?

YOU

Every place I think is the place I got hurt, I go
to. Then I realize I must've got hurt before I

was there. Cuz I carry it with me all the time. Probably happened when I was little. When I was 8.

SAINT

Shit always happens when you 8.

YOU

Just the fucking shits.

SAINT

Heard Kanye in here.

YOU

For fuck's sake.

SAINT

Could be a good thing.

YOU

In what world?

SAINT

They could forget about us a little, let us stay out longer.

YOU

Right.

SAINT

A nigga can dream.

YOU

Unfortunately, yes.

You think of other buildings that don't have windows. Strip clubs finally come to mind. If the DMV has windows, they are so poorly tended to, it feels like they don't. Courts.

You've tried to read while in here, but the words hover just above the page and scramble. Nothing about your brain feels like your brain. You imagine yourself a stripper, climbing relentlessly on a pole and hitting your head over and over again on the ceiling. Now you're a deer as stripper, walking delicately on the glass runway. Now the runway is a highway. You stand in front of the headlights, the money being thrown as your body is about to become corpse. And the money gets thrown, becomes a cloud, windswept. The spots on your pelt fall off. You don't know what light could blind you so viscerally you stop being able to move. Then you remember you've been in this position before. Your mind severing connection to your arms, the two of them gumming up like spit, useless. You were 8, but it was more than that moment, those events. It was the way nothing changed after. The way your mom continued to look at you, the way your dad begged for your time, the way your sister looked up. They didn't know, or couldn't have known, or knew and thought you just got over it. The money around your hooves is now an ocean, the one close to the hospital you currently live in, close enough anyway. Some men put money in you ears, big as they are now. It's hard to walk off the stage, being that it would be a leap. You leap. The money, river-like, flows and follows you out. The headlights don't materialize into a truck. You're just free. And now what do you do. And now who are you even. As always, as in childhood, there are two of you. Bearded and shaved. Gloss and gruff. In the wake of yourself, you are most acutely not human at all.

SAINT

I'm not about to get in trouble just cuz you
want someone to hold your hand.

YOU

It's okay.

SAINT

Did you even want that?

YOU

No. I really thought I was right.

SAINT

You more fucked up than me then.

YOU

The other black guy that's in here is like really fucking smart.

SAINT

Hard when it backfires.

YOU

Can you sleep?

SAINT

Haven't. When they check in on you that much.

YOU

Don't they know that? And what could we be doing anyway?

SAINT

Weird shit? I dunno.

YOU

I think spying on folks when they sleep is
weird shit.

SAINT

For sure.

YOU

I don't see the white lizards anymore.

SAINT

You think they were real?

YOU

I-- fuck it. I left all my shit there. I left every-
one I loved there.

SAINT

She might forgive you.

YOU

You don't know her.

SAINT

What you think they did with your shit?

YOU

Part of me hopes they burned it. I don't like
the idea of folks using stuff that had my hands
in it, my life in it.

SAINT

They calling us back in.

YOU
Think we could get out of here? Like break
out?

SAINT
Why would you even want that? You keep
coming back in.

Saint walks back inside, leaving you near the makeshift
garden of only succulents and some rosemary. You smell
the rosemary. Another way to feel. Whatever you were be-
fore, your grace is in starting from nothing now. The deer
you are is still walking home, on the sidewalks to avoid
traffic. Money falling out of her gait. You hope she doesn't
get hit by a car. She doesn't quite fit. You hope they don't.
The deer named Two keeps walking. You go back inside.

he climbs into your bed touches your nipple each one you
remind him of people who are distinctly not you maybe
you are becoming them a cousin from New Orleans with a
gold tooth in her top row a triple D bosom sweat in creases
you've never held moisture her hair electrocuted and Don
King'd outward I see an outhouse fire and biscuits she's
warmth and pussy and lipstick and grace from God church-
es and crutches and a too-loud laugh you are becoming her
swollen ankles day dresses calico words you've never said
handkerchiefs maybe once she went to Mexico all the cig-
arettes and her teeth yellow as old paper from them in this
way you are already her like an old letter or a tea stained
new letter made to look old she has a name that is at least
80 years older than you will ever be she smells of pork
rinds and sweet potato and men their spit musk and all al-
ways barefoot never pregnant so he can be the only focus
she reads the bible for the hot parts the sodom the gammo-
rah the Delilah the wine the sacked cities the salt she lives
in a one room shack she is some kind of God and you have
a different name you are needy you are desperate you shud-
der in the night you take medication it's required you drink
port by the bottle you drink quickly every man who touch-
es you is somehow your father you say what you're feel-
ing you are regarded as pathetic and in need of pity your
breasts are bigger than you expected and ask too much of
you who are you anyway aren't you supposed to be her
swamp understood roux ready to boil the baby boomer's
dream of comfort if the boomer is raised a man and man
like strapping and emotional underneath that onyx demand
that primer for a solider yes eradicate the skin of your father
who is somehow always present in the corner as you make
what is called love to a man who begs from you his own
mother your father is a judge the robes the presentation the
law abiding the God the God the God a certain perfection

the man above and inside you is none of these things but cannot see your face somehow or ever designs and decides you a person who is long since dead you hear her name thru his lips as he cums on your leg he finds satisfaction he expresses every fear every illness borne of anxiety you absorb it you are a black hole you don't bring enough care to the occasion you are just playing hard to get you are just hard to get you are gotten and forsaken there are many people you no longer speak to he is not one of them be more expand you picture that her eyes the her you are becoming are big in the circular way like a as a whatever they big and can encompass all of him every rejection a salve is born in you who is not you but is woman after woman he's loved before you you have become a catalog a demographic unto yourself he sits you down in the mornings to discuss how inferior you were in the nights how you demurred and curled away from him & it is good that he hates so much of you that he craves and shouldn't you want your man to want you you should only be angry if he doesn't reach out hand over hand to nipple covered nipple he doesn't hear when you say no under the blankets under the pillows you are becoming now furniture what are you now and what have you been he wants and wants and is hungry give you to him you are a carcass after all you have been dead for decades you are not you you are the woman the women he's already lusted for so fuck it just open wide why doncha just commence and capitulate and contrive give it to him so you ain't gotta hear no bullshit in the morning he is the morning the daylight a cosmos he is a prediction a star gaze a theory realized he is your man your partner your son somehow just as he is your father somehow a face looking into a pond and seeing his reflection and wanting nothing else except for a body underneath the mirror why are there no bodies underneath the mirrors sex sex sex to be inside of a body you aren't and you already done fucked ain't chu being women who aren't your name for him do this in remembrance of him a tithe an offering surely there have been better have been more Issac and Abraham and all and that's Old Testament that's his upbringing the brimstone the fire you are not the fire you smolder and ember and might as well be ocean dwelling to be unseen is a hatred to be seen ferocious and in his gaze you are both now you are eclipsed you are a hippie he calls you you are his youth if only he was 30 years younger if only you had never been born you want to slim your waistline you want to get free as they say you want the ring off the gesture blown and he corrals you into a bedroom anonymous pours the champagne even if it's just the last time he says and you curl up and into the last time you are slimmer your stomach hurts less it is over and your cigarettes at the ready you are no longer his dream the painting of the woman with her blouse upturned the wrists curved can't you see me without me can't you want me without me a lover of a woman who loves women a pegged joke how could you have made it work when you were exempt from desire an often asexual a deer in the headlights as they say my goodness they sure do talk a lot don't they you washed his back you said his prayers you drank his cognac you hear his stories you were his bitch he was your bitch it was in a way even steven ya dig & it was good the way God is the way God says so but you can't say who exactly wrote the bible cuz no one talks about that and you can't say if he was a bad man or a good man or even your man when the shit breaks down because you didn't see him enough times a week to make him your boyfriend so what did it all matter anyway if we all become dust if Moses wrote the shit on those tablets and even they became dust if all this lust is for naught because the black holes are encroaching if you are never even you because you are too busy being too many other people then what did it matter if he was good if you were good if it was good it was so busy trying not to die

& everyone was alive is not always a good thing some
men are good some men buy back the block and thousands
fly out to watch as they walk with 6 men carrying them
a corpse in a box in Ghana they dance underneath while
holding the body in my family they burn the body and scat-
ter let nothing be good but all be grown my aunt wants to
die and become a tree there's lots of ways to get out of this
body I do it all the time my therapist says when my eyes
roll up to the windowsill that I'm leaving myself behind
and it's better it's clever to not remember how a distant
she touched me while I was wearing my mother's blue slip
while I was too young to understand much beyond a sub-
title what a person was really saying underneath what they
were saying it's shocking that I've gone this long misun-
derstanding myself but when compared to everyone else
with a day job I'm part of a club a band of folks who refuse
to read the fine print I can't stay in my I long enough to
make an impression becoming you the distance a comfort
you're floating on the ceiling of anyplace in the Southern
tradition if you paint a ceiling blue it wards off the haints
the ghost bodies the not quite here's of which you are al-
ways at least halfway one since you were 8 an age that is
usually for shit for most when you went to Ghana you were
stung by a morning mosquito the kind that carry dengue
your blood getting slower underneath your skin and here
you are again not necessarily yourself so far from your own
subject position can't you just say I am in pain I am in a
hospital with a bag of saline above my head I am so far
from home I smell the water between each continent that I
am unhappy because being alone relinquishes me from my
narcissist counterpart that I am codependent and suckling
away on a teat far gone no just say it was you put it on
someone else you the version of I that is easier to stomach
you farther away and whoever I need you to be you are

alive and that is not always a good thing decomposing is
noble an organic pursuit at least a silent one more or less
and what did anyone even mean the first time someone said
the words more or less what were they exactly going for
the middle ground the boundary the amount that doesn't
make someone grate their teeth someone you mean you
you mean I I mean hey buy me a drink why doncha give
a girl some ambition some drive an incentive program ba-
sically to be dead doesn't really disturb me it's just that I
would finally quite finally be alone that bugs me out alone
and no one else's problems to compose me to define me a
compass of freaky sort no more someone big climbing into
my corpus and claiming it a makeshift home my narcissist
my dom a you a he a she a they a hand on my throat is
the requirement I like when someone makes it harder and
harder for me to breathe when someone you they plays a
recording of their voice and has me listen to it for edit do
you get a word in edgewise do they know anything about
you other than your asides are you a co star no the corpse
star but the nigga delivering the eulogy what do the nu-
tritional facts say what's the carbohydrates the number is
smaller than your age your age is always a point of conver-
sation for the boomers who feel you won't die before them
they consume you don't you want to be consumed don't
I fuck it's hard to smile in a mirror it's hard to say I need
I scrape I jive I burrow and borrow I am Sicilian in some
parts of me and I need to know more about that vendettas
and whatnot the chapels the streets gone clean of violence
the violence I need to know how to stay inside this suit of
skin you can't I can't but I who that just wait quit it now
no dance come on you no I wait fuck just fuck him then if
you're so worried about being seen but I don't want dick
but you might but she can't but she's not a she but she can't
give herself a name but I need what need you aren't real
you aren't even here she takes a pull and walks a few steps
further down the street she is alive and I and she is

so where does that leave you back at Cape Coast the secu-
rity guard takes accounting of your arms the hair growing
from them assesses your legs must do the same the line
trailing your stomach making halves of it the small delin-
eation on your upper lip coming down off the sides squar-
ing your chin your eyebrows able to be combed and made
emphasis and out of your head an abundance he says to
you never shave and you realize your whole life's been a
racket a controlled notion of body commanding that hair
ain't a thing and it seems small cosmetic this gesture to-
ward selfhood you remember the connotations of hair how
it meant dirt in high school how it meant more blk some-
how intimidating too much brick house smelly unbeautiful
what it asked of you was pools of water in bathtubs full of
shorn and blood and soap you were closer to some iteration
of sewage and you couldn't tell for what to avoid recogni-
tion broken plastic razors littering your feet pockets of fat
now greased and hairless were you about to be eaten is a
fair question out from your nipples too there was and is no
escape from this highlight your mother said all that hair
was for protection and you'd have thought it could do a
better job you're not giving the hair enough credit remem-
ber that time on that beach with that guy and that darkness
and that shack that was an under-built bathroom and how
he rammed you against that concrete wall and kept trying
to unzip your pants and y'all were essentially physically
fighting and you said no but who cared and then that Rasta
dude jumped in at the crucial moment and said wah gwan
so like yea
the hair helped you then

THAT TIME ON THE BEACH WITH THAT GUY

5'7, rhinestone studded belt that spells out NERD, slick back hair with gel, the generic from a CVS type store, a muscle tee, tucked into the belt and the jeans that are very, very tight fitting, slim, and all, he'd have a vape if it was the year vapes became the thing which this year is too early for that to be true, a douche, mostly Lebanese and employs many Ghanians, a white supremacy of sorts, the club that's only open Wednesday nights, the back of it, near the men's restrooms

THAT GUY
But I want to.

YOU
Huh?

THAT GUY
America. That right?

YOU
America. That's right.

THAT GUY
Your whole life?

YOU
Not dead yet, so sure.

THAT GUY
Yikes. So morbid.

YOU
You the one brought up life.

THAT GUY

Exactly. Life.

YOU

I think we're saying the same thing.

THAT GUY

Shots. Jameson?

YOU

Eh.

THAT GUY

Something more…

YOU

Of the area.

THAT GUY

Cane spirits?

YOU

As in sugar?

THAT GUY

It's what we got here.

YOU

Cuz of slavery.

THAT GUY

No. Cuz it grows here.

YOU

Slavery can grow.

THAT GUY
Hard to be the one that went away.

YOU
Excuse me?

THAT GUY
That's what you are. One of the ones who went away.

YOU
You ain't even from here.

THAT GUY
My whole life.

YOU
If you die tonight.

THAT GUY
If you ain't have such a fat ass I wouldn't be talking to you.

YOU
Get the shots.

That Guy goes to get the shots. The club has typical club features: disco ball poorly utilized, multicolored laser-pointed lights, leather couches that either get too deep or not deep enough, wet bars, stairs to and out of sunken-in rooms. It's the first time you're at a club and most of the people are black-- different than how you're black, as in, not brown or gradations of brown-- nah, just black. And from Ghana black. Know where their ancestors are from black. You hadn't fully realized that you could be black and know where your ancestors are from until now, until living here, where are constantly reminded that you are obrunni-- a white person. That passport and brown skin make you white, exactly the things that make you black where you're from. That Guy is in the crowded line to get you shots and you don't know why there always has to be a That Guy for the evening to have been epic. What you want is to be alone, cry at the expense of your life-- the fundamental nature of being from nowhere exactly.

                        THAT GUY
Got you a double.

                          YOU
How generous.

                        THAT GUY
Why don't you shave?

                          YOU
What?

                        THAT GUY
You just got like all this fucking hair on your
body.

                          YOU
Thanks.

                        THAT GUY
You some kinda dyke?

                          YOU
                    Some kind, yea.

> THAT GUY
>> For real?

They down said shots.

> THAT GUY
> I gotta go to the bathroom.

> YOU
> Bet.

> THAT GUY
> Come with me.

> YOU
> Stop being to typical.

> THAT GUY
> Calling me basic?

> YOU
> Not basic, just obvious.

> THAT GUY
> You got nice tits.

> YOU
> I been thinking of having them removed.

> THAT GUY
> Huh?

YOU
Why is your belt so big?

THAT GUY
Come with me.

That Guy takes your hand and walks you to the men's bathroom. It's your third day here, you're turning 21 soon, your cousin died a few weeks back, shot in a drive by at the McDonald's on Crenshaw & 43rd. It bothers you, that you get to be alive while he gets to be, God knows, on another leg of this whole journey. Not that you want to be dead-- it's got a name, survivor's guilt. He was training to be an EMT, save people on the ground floor and what do you do? Tell stories? Bang it out in club bathrooms? Go on dates with women, make out, get triggered by who molested you when you were 8, then cry in their arms, explaining nothing? You know your purpose, but it feels insignificant and frivolous compared to that of your cousin. You and your dad went to Cedars the day he died. When you walked in, there were already Welcome Home balloons in the lobby-- every doctor said he was looking good, was gonna pull thru. Doctors shouldn't be allowed to employ language, ever, at all. Your aunt, the most hilarious and cackle-ready woman you know, is sitting under a wreath of balloons, her face smacked by a cognitive dissonance, "My son is dead." You go into the room he is laying. Crowds of plastic bags with dregs of blood fill the corners-- you never knew his blood type. Such intimacies are usually never known. At least 70 bags, everywhere in the room is sparse and full. There's his girlfriend, wailing over him. You approach, touch his forehead. You don't know why, but you are disturbed that he doesn't move underneath your hand, adjust to the connection, make himself more at ease. Then you know why. He is dead. It's really so simple, the release of all this life. But the simplicity has left you a zombie, unable to move your arms much in defense, unable to walk away from what is obviously a terrible idea. That Guy shuts the door.

                    YOU
This is gross.

                    THAT GUY
What, me?

                    YOU
Yes, you.

                    THAT GUY
What you say?

                    YOU
No, just, people shit in here.

                    THAT GUY
And fuck in here.

                    YOU
Not me.

                    THAT GUY
You want to.

                    YOU
You want to--

                    THAT GUY
That's what I said--

YOU

I have to find my friend.

THAT GUY

What friend?

That Guy makes a good point, even though he doesn't know it. She's not really your friend, but is a product of the kind of relationships you're used to-- codependent, narcissistic bonds, "I can't do anything without you..." and the like. It's the one cultivated with your dad, the special buddy-buddy-ness, the one your mom described as, "you two have your own language," another moment language betrays you. You think all relationships are like this, and that if they are not, you are doing something wrong or just got a break for some divine reason. Because of this, you have a litany of platonic romances, always on the brink of sexual consumption, because it is erotic, this level of control over someone else. You are always in the submissive, the borderline to their Godness. You want to find her anyway because she knows y'all address and you'd never be forgiven if you left her here without telling her in person (instead of say, over the phone, in text message), that you just had to leave, That Guy was getting to aggressive, it was late.

YOU

Seriously, lemme just see where she's at. I'll be right back.

THAT GUY

I'll go with you.

YOU

Um. Okay.

THAT GUY
Shit I'm so fucking hard.

You unlock the door and barrel out into the club. You still want to tend to That Guy because hey, he did buy you those drinks after all, and aren't you programmed to accommodate?
You find your friend clustered in some corner with another anonymous man, older, balder, but the same deal. She wants to go to the beach, there's a concert or something, it's special, real authentic Ghana, come on, we have to go.
You get into the car with That Guy, she with her guy. You're off.

YOU
Why do you have a 1/5 of Henny in your car?

THAT GUY
I'm into tourism.

YOU
Ah.

THAT GUY
We could just go to my place.

YOU
I don't know where you stay at.

THAT GUY
You'd find out when you got there.

YOU
You sound mad.

THAT GUY
I'm allowed. Can't tell what's good with you.

YOU
Are we almost there?

THAT GUY
Just a couple more streets.

YOU
Bet.

THAT GUY
What are you, anyway?

YOU
Like am I a lamp or a couch--

THAT GUY
Don't be a dick.

YOU
I don't get you.

THAT GUY
You like, a dude or what?

YOU
Does it matter?

THAT GUY
I mean if you got a dick I'm not here for it.

YOU
I don't have a dick.

THAT GUY

Aight.

That Guy parks his Audi at beach parking. You smell the water, what else can you do, it's right there and you can't control that sense, like hearing, the queerness of being unable to dictate what goes in those two orifices, unlike your eyes, which can close whenever you need an escape. Your friend is already there, walking in the sand heavy way down to the beach with her guy, older, balder, whatever. They find another blanket of midnight to curl up in. You realize you and That Guy are walking past all that's lit-- the bar, wooden tables on the beach, the pool tables, the Rastafarians, which you realize Ghana has in large population, black dudes from the islands who wanted to go "back home," this is home. Halie Selassie and all that. You admire it, the conviction that a place you've never lived in could become home based solely on history, on what the books and stories and ache in your body says.

You were born in Los Angeles, so far removed from a piece of your history. You'd feel like a poser if you became a Rasta, so you smile at them instead. That Guy keeps walking you somewhere and you realize he is walking you, your legs are octopus boneless and all of you is just infatuated with that smell. The water. The water that took you away. The passage. It was here, that all that went down. The first ships carrying cargo to become you.

YOU

Where are we?

THAT GUY

They still building it.

YOU
Is this another fucking bathroom.

THAT GUY
Shut up, aight?

That Guy starts taking off things that belong to you. Your pants, the zipper on them, your panties. It's all coming apart. You push away, you say,

YOU
Nah, please, I'm really not--

THAT GUY
Then why'd you come here with me?

YOU
My friend--

THAT GUY
Fuck your friend.

YOU
Come on, man, just chill, okay--

THAT GUY
Shut up you'll like it--

YOU
No--

THAT GUY
Quit playin--

                    YOU
I'm not, just stop, okay--

                  THAT GUY
    You'll like it, you just don't know it yet.

                  RASTA DUDE
                   Wah gwan?

And you just run. Some dude, who looks like a Rasta you
saw on the shore moments ago, pops his head in. Maybe he
saw how suspect your interaction with That Guy looked,
each step a charge toward horror. You see yourself in the
water that you now stand so close to. There's moonlight
but it's not romantic. It does its job-- it illuminates. You
know what was about to happen to you. What all already
happened to you. But the violation, on some level, feels
normal. And that's what makes you hold yourself, arm in
activated arm, no longer boneless. Why are you used to the
things you're used to? The Rasta Dude is still talking to
That Guy, and you see a cultural exchange-- the Rasta who
wanted to come home to ancestral Ghana, the Lebanese
dude who wanted to profit off the land and Ghana was the
obvious choice. Am I the land? Ancestral and capital still?
You need a ride home, there are no taxis running this late.
You turn around. They're both gone. You walk back to the
bar, where That Guy sits, pissed and drinking another shot.

                  THAT GUY
    Why'd you do that?

                    YOU
I need a ride home.
Are you good to drive?

                                                        89

THAT GUY
You want a ride or not?

YOU
Okay.

Your friend walks with her guy, older, balder, still, to his car. You each get rides home. She looks happy, satiated. She doesn't ask you how your night went, how was That Guy, and she doesn't for days after. She never does. And that's fine. You get home. He lets you out the car, not saying a word. You hope he isn't memorizing your address, you hope he deletes your number from his contact. You go inside your dorm, your roommate from Spelman, an HBCU, already asleep, tidy, in her bed. Your eyes close. Two hours later, you are up, puking furiously. You do this until all that comes up is water. Your stomach is stitching in pain, something inside that shouldn't be. It wasn't the alcohol, or anything That Guy may have thought of putting in it. It was the water. You always have to boil it. The water doesn't agree with you.

The I has disintegrated. Cannot be stood inside of. The you is unstable, fissures and infrastructure collapse imminent. But the body is still intact. Where can the personhood disperse to? That final critical option, that one can't come back from. I and you becoming and unbecoming unto this. The practice, since the age of 8, shifting out of skin and into anything else. The ancestral trauma has knocked out the identity— didn't ultimately matter the geographical location, the here. Or the who, opposite, inside of, occasionally. What can be called, too much. Too much has happened. The self retires. Adopts a combination of the name, the cultivated name from practicing being outside the self: Two.

Two has this recurring dream, every night, a ritual. They feel around in their mouth with their tongue and a critical tooth, one in the front, close to the people Two'd encounter, falls out. Spits it out like a sunflower seed and then all the rest start raining out they mouth, having been mistaken that one tooth was more important than the others. Sometimes the teeth Two spits out aren't even teeth. They were when lodged in their gums, but once out the mouth and into the hand, they are the most pedestrian of objects; a key chain, a class ring, a shark tooth emblem on a penny you put in a slot at an amusement park. Garbage treasure, items that could be cherished or repellent or most often both. Two wonder what that meant they was made of, as a human person. Made of the shit you should throw away? Or if their teeth could be shapeshifting— was Two even what their mirror dictated back to them? Whenever Two wakes up from this dream, they feel around in their mouths, a return to sanity; these are my teeth and they are in my mouth. Two wondered when the recurrence started. When their father would sing to them before sleep?

Or when their father would play the Ken Burn's Civil War tapes before sleep? Or was this dream the progression of Two's other recurring dream— the one where they got sleep paralysis underneath their parent's wedding quilt, the one with the names of every member of their family sewn into it expect their own because they weren't alive then, and their English professor enters the room, a shadow, his pants bulging lewdly, to stand over Two's bed, laughing?

The dream is never more interesting than what it represents; anxiety. At the time, Two didn't know Saint was from East St. Louis and that that's different than the rest of St. Louis and that he was anything more than Two's late night Landshark delivery man. Two had ordered sushi and waited for the order to complete, receiving a call from a number native to St. Louis, the voice on the end of the line complaining that he couldn't find the house and Two had to understand, their house being entirely consumed by kudzu vines, an invasive species, carnivorous and not native to the South, but here all the same, the most human of plants, by its nature to eat. This kind of insatiable humanity makes it hard to see the number on the front of Two's building, 746. The door being mostly glass, Two sees theyself before they see Saint, shuffling on the sidewalk, plastic bag in hand, phone to left ear.

An Oxford University Police car passes behind Saint, Saint from Saint Louis, East, and Two has decided tonight that between the University Police, the Lafayette County Police and the Oxford City Police that they all took the job just so they could whip a Dodge Challenger and get paid for doing so. Drive around in their tiny town and repeatedly drive past their ex-girlfriend's new apartment, accelerating and blood rising into his white, now pink face like it would during their sex, which doesn't happen anymore since she dumped him and took up work at the Oxford University Bank, passing her time watching HGTV during business hours, remolding in her mind a house she and her new man don't yet own. Two is judgmental when it comes to police, white police, but black police too. Watching Saint confused and knocking each door that isn't theirs, in tandem with the police car slowly pulling up in front of him, everything in Two's body wants to reach out and grab Saint, ushering him indoors, safety. If Two could control the kudzu, they would carry Saint in that way, their arms stringing outward and toward him, a Medusa moment, curling him and enveloping him, a tree finally saving a black man instead of being the life he dies on. Two walks out their front door to the porch, screams,

Right here!

And the police car goes off. Past Saint's car, which is white, the way Two's car is white— the cheapest model on the lot because you can see it miles away, insurance purposes. Two noticed that Saint was unusually shiny. It wasn't summer. He wasn't sweating. But there was a shine to him, as if inherited, like the earrings in his ears only embedded in his body. Shiny like you know he has a mini-hair brush in his back pocket and the moment he leaves your porch, he's going to start brushing the fuck out of his head until the waves wave right. A whole ocean to tend to on his head. Shoes as white as his car, toothbrushed to the glory of small bones that will stay in your mouth, the kind Two doesn't have. Saint walks up to Two's porch, all kinds of clink and clank sounds emitting from his pockets. The keys, the hair brush, the wallet, the phone, the grinder, the weed canister, the lighter, the swisher sweets, the Tic Tacs. Loose change? Do folks still carry loose change? Coins?

Two doesn't know why they even give a shit about this dude. They have their own shit to contend with— even the smallest nic in the fabric of their day, the statues. In Oxford, there are two Confederate statues, one on Ole Miss campus, the other in the town square and for the first time today, Two wanted to know to what are those statues saluting? They're looking in such a clear direction, everything about their posture feels riddled with intention, but to who are they giving their allegiance? This was fixating Two, likely because they didn't want their mind to wander to other events— how their mother continues to fall into near-miss accidental deaths, as if their family now has triggered some long buried ancestral curse. Or how Two recently has begun to see and hear things that likely are only there in their eyes, their ears. The deer outside their home, it was speaking to Two. Surely. It happened. But what is happening? Time, even? Two was getting heavy into string theory and only just now concerned that they would end up like that other chick who moved to Oxford and was left in a spare room listening to Infinite Jest audio book on repeat for days, not washing her body or clothes, a particular stink wafting from her corner of the old house. And Two lived in an old house. Plantation style, which did not escape them, being a black body.

When it rained, only in Two's room would the water seep from outside into their walls, melting down their James Baldwin and Toni Morrison post cards carefully tacked up. Two constantly feels like their space is becoming entirely water, washing away. That this house doesn't want them here. That their body feels the same, kicking them out of theyself. Saint rings the doorbell, not seeing Two just to the right of him, toying with a cigarette. Two lets him wait to see them. Saint does.

Two pictured the bodies behind Saint's body as he stood in the threshold between porch and doorway. His football coach at Ole Miss, a leathered white, grunting with an ox-barritone at his field of black players, all running their fastest to him, for before-sunrise drills. The bitter notion of Saint's two busted knees soon after, a product of abiding direction. His hands gripped around the neck of the plastic bag, surely, they were his grandmother's hands, worn and wrinkled and delicately calloused. His nail beds deep as Two's, what their own grandmother hoped would be their inheritance, prayed that Two had their mother and grandmother's hands, womanly, was the wish. Two's hands were that with an addendum— the hair on their knuckles. For a time, Two thought to shave it off, their hands then being too much like their father's, screaming with hair. A violence, this hair. Snatching Two away from their woman-body, that felt true and unture all at once. Pity that was the smallest real estate the hair converged on; soon the women of Two's family would find that they was an unending supply of hair, the body entirely full of it. Two never felt farther from their mother than the moment Two tried to shave their legs. Back to the reverberation from Saint's body: Two feels as though this person in front of them is known to them, somehow. In a glitch, some ancestral trauma will reveal their relationship. A black man in front of a black someone. A woman body, but not a woman. It's happened before, surely. Surely.

Saint handed Two their plastic bag— an order of sushi, and given the town, maybe this was a poor choice of cuisine, given that it was land locked and not a town sushi was particularly known for— and Two's hand met his, fingers and knuckles colliding. Their body next to his— a thought jettisoning through Two's mind. Why? Two felt their mind dulling to the depravity of a rock, just a thing things happened to. And Two wanted in this moment for Saint to happen to them. As if they'd already been together in a room with no windows. Or saved from each other on a beach in Ghana. This was a man that had happened before to Two and would keep happening, a pattern of reincarnation, a spirit surrounding its site of haunting. Two could've said nothing, taken their food and closed the door. But didn't. Instead the hand that met his hand held on, a second. Another second. Two didn't understand. Maybe it was because Two was living with a couple of white folks from the South, who would verbally fight and chase each other through their home, shouting,

There used to be flowers here! It used to be beautiful!

And other things that screamed unrequited love. Basical-
ly, *The Real World* meets Tennessee Williams. And may-
be it was just too many white people, too much of noth-
ing close to the body Two inhabited, too many buckets
of cigarette butts and ashes and Bud Light cans squashed
and red cups in the kudzu. It might have been that Two
was looking for someone— shiny and wave kept, black
and grandmother-handed. Two was far from home and
close to a certain understanding. And father away from
their body than when the day began. It was a process,
this walking further and further away from theyself.
They were good at it. As opposed to yelling, which they
did not excel.

Do you wanna, uh, come inside?

Huh?

*I mean, I don't have enough to share but. Come inside?
Have a beer?*

I don't drink.

Or smoke up with me?

Saint wouldn't have described Two as desperate, even
though that's exactly the word to be used here. Who
knows what Saint saw in Two to go inside the house
wrapped in carnivorous vegetation.

Sure.

Two was intent on being an offering equipped with demands; a hymn. A sun setting and appealing the sky to get purple for a moment, before the moon and her whole agenda. *If you're gonna do this, you're gonna do this,* said a voice somewhere within Two, a woman in a red dress, braying, almost. A command? Two brushed at their ear, shaking it off. But abiding. Two knows to obey. *Let down your hair, move your arms wider so the muscle tee you're wearing shows off more side boob,* said another red dress wearing voice from Two's head. Saint followed Two through the front room into their room, the walls still wet from the storm that morning, the photos of black writers Two loved wrinkled and puckered against the wall. Saint took out his swisher sweets (Two was right), his grinder, his weed. He needed a place to roll, Two escorts the both of them outside, the patio that wraps around the back of the house.

They sit. Saint sits too. The swisher sweets are broken out, the tobacco inside slowly carved out and shaken clear. Two remembers, seeing the shuck and tender of this practice, their father, a question asked before sleep, *What do you dream?* About my teeth falling out. Then them not being my teeth. Just products of the world. Is Two merely a product? To be bought, sold, discarded? At once, Two is no longer on their porch, but manacled on a ship, debris and human stick enveloping them, can't breathe in but for the smell. A white man above them, resembling their grandfather, blonde hairs growing out of his arms, shoulders, his ears, whip-ready and yelling, yelling what? A salute— to what? What do these men salute to? It's above his head, taller than most buildings a man could make— so not man made, then what? Their God? So ephemeral, that doesn't satisfy Two, their wrists churning in the rusting manacles. A tooth shakes itself free, their body is paralyzed underneath the shadow of this white arm and arm above them, Two preparing to

become whatever his hands will make them. Then not—
Two is on the back porch in the year they are in, sushi on
the porch table, turning.

The porch was framed by a situation of magnolia trees,
which to Two had rapidly become non-beautiful. They
couldn't hold any smell of a bloom from that tree in their
memory— maybe it had a smell, but Two wouldn't rec-
ognize it. Every house Two had ever lived in up until this
moment had a mandatory magnolia tree in front of it. No
matter the state in this country, the magnolia was always
true. Two had decided magnolias were death flowers, a
crossroads unto themselves, a procession of a flower.
Since Two was eight, their resentment for the flowers
smelled more memorable than the flower itself. But Two
never owned the land the tree grew out of, and maybe
that was to do with it. What resentment does to a nose,
that primal recall.

Where are you from?

East St. Louis.

Oh, Saint Louis is—

Nah. East.

Oh. Where you from before East Saint Louis?

Georgia. My family from there.

Sharecroppers?

All that.

Then East Saint Louis— work in a factory or something?

Chrysler.

Land parts to car parts.

They the few blk folk got the 40?

Yea. No mule tho.

Two wanted to know what does a black family do with 40 acres given to them, but now felt too shy to ask. This stranger was becoming known to them— why did they let a stranger into their home? How lonely could a bitch get before they started letting any ole body into their space? Because their home was environmentally expelling Two regardless, why not have a last hurrah. Go down with the ship. Everything goes back to a ship, in Two's mind, an ancestral glitch. On a practical level, Two understood some of their own actions. The desire to leave their own body works best when it is into another body— through their time, their touch, their words. Whatever you can cling to, it becomes a raft— a stranger no longer strange. Talking with Saint quieted the voices and sights in Two's head— a stranger can do that. Who are they anyway. What do you owe them— nothing. But there was a charge here, a sense Two couldn't shake that someone they did owe Saint something, that he was previously known. That his name could change and revert back, that he had been several people before now, all known to Two.

Do y'all still have it? The 40? Do y'all?

Huh. I don't know.

And Saint became again the black man Two was trained

all they life how to love; bold somehow, dead already somehow, and forgetful as fuck. Trained to appease, to smile brightly at, to make comfortable their body in the warmth of their space, open always to him, whoever the him was. Who was the first man, the first black man, Two was conditioned to take care of? To mother, though Two was not and likely would never mother any children, or parent, as the gender specificity would endear of language? Their father, clearly. Once, Two had asked their father where he grew up. He proceeded to draw a building, old and decrepit, that is now El Museo del Barrio. This was his home for a short time, but this is the home he decided to draw for Two, and Two's heart retired. They felt the impulse, the muscle, to console and uplift their father, say it was okay that he endured all he endured because wasn't he here now? And he'd sigh, an exhale full of every bitterness, resentment, self-doubt, self-hate, abandonment unresolved (and never would be resolved because the person doing the abandoning had long since died), and make some kind of face, suggesting that sure, maybe it was all worth it, Two not understanding the maybe because wasn't their father happy to have them in his life? Two would sometimes ask this of him, sometimes not, depending on how loud and how long the sigh went for. Later, Two would discover that part of the sigh included Two's half brother, a person Two had no idea existed and now they were 20, the aforementioned brother 11 years older. And there was another man Two felt the inextricable pull to care for; a man they'd never met who had their face.

What was Two's standards for family? If a man is your family, he gets all of your care, all of your energy, all of your good parts— the Mammy-making of black femmes and black women, and this befell Two since the moment their body was outwardly discernible from men. And there was no labor for the man to do— just to talk, pontificate on their life, their woes, their women troubles, their aches, their pains, their car breakdowns, their job breakdowns, their strength or lack thereof, their passion or lack thereof, their receding hairlines, their muscles come to fat, their fat come to muscle, their needs, their wants, their secrets, their hopes, their degradation, their worst nightmares, their mothers, their fathers, their dysfunctions, their desperation, their misspelled words and misused time, their words unsaid, their calls unmade, their violence, their attempts at violence, their refrain from violence and the soliloquy that follows their restraint, their lust, their hunger, their compulsions, their tics, their fixations, their attractions, their sweat, their seed, their milestones, their traditions, named and unnamed, their delights, their hard-earned tears, the occasion the tears make themselves known, their narcissism, does that go without saying, their claims, their property, their chattel, their ships, how are we back at ships, the constellations lead back to the same slavery, the creases in their pants, their attempts at living forever, their claim on youth, their death wish, their Oedipal complexes, kill the father fuck the mother, their kill the father fuck the mother, their wives as mothers, their mothers as Gods, their Gods as forsaken, their rehab should they take the step, their higher power, (themselves) their villainy, their heroism, the both sides of the same coin frustration, their coins, their cash, their fat stacks, their cheddar, their tenderness, their try a little tenderness, their tactics, their belonging, their renewed vows, their children, their other children, which child decides who's the real family, their choices, their refusal to make their own choices, their hatred, their adoration, their gifts, their swan songs, their favorite TV shows, their wish fulfillments, their call to arms, their arms, their unending suffering, their surgeries, their appendixes, their lungs, their hearts, their brains, their clots and blockages, their pills and recovery, their teeth, longer and well tended to, their smell, their musk, their gruff and grit, their ambition, their desperation, their hustle, their occupation, their vocation, what they are called to, their hobbies, what they try to keep alive, how they try to subtly or overtly kill you, their patterns, same shit a different day, their journals, their well worn shoes, their slow songs, their multiple languages, their one language, their lineage, the hair on their arms, blonde as the patriarch, fields of blonde in the line of black men, their always stories, the ones told at the same gesture, every time told, their histories, how it all went down up til now, their line, son of their son, blood of their blood, the next heir, their title, Mr. Dr. Esq. etc, their instability, their denial, their disappearance, their long walk home, their women unloved, their women, their women, their women, ever-changing women even when the marriage stays in tact, the women of their imagination, the women of their past, the women on the street that glance their way, the women in traffic, the women at the DMV that flirt at the end of their shifts, the women at restaurants, the women, the women, the women, their vice, their stress, their white men who hold them by the teeth, still a slave in so many regards and who are the black women they come to, hoping to feel bigger than? They were like Two. Every generation.

Two knew more of men that any education could've provided and, they thought, learned to survive them. But here Two was now, inviting strange men into their home, men that of course are familiar if they have the same relationship to black femmes or black women or a black whoever that looks even the slightest soft. Anyone with that education would look, would feel, would be their family. Whatever family meant. Two wanted to tell Saint what they could do, if their mind was lost from them for long enough. That they could become a deer. But would Saint think that was so insane, would he even believe them? What in his life could ever make him become not-human? Did he also have this power? This curse?

As Two looked at Saint, his answer having just spilled out his mouth, *huh? I don't know,* they began to see him— calves not skin enclosed, but scaled, a prehistoric quality, a hardness. A curvature of harsh grooves making up his back, grey and leather firm, leather weary. Instead of his spine, visible and harsh the way it is on most humans, pathetically accessible, his was sheltered iron-borne— a shield of sorts made up his back, rounded and with the potential to round further and further inward, making ball of the body. His hands, still rolling the blunt to be, the nails extending further and further outward, pointed, as an auntie of Two's would have it, going to the nail salon and adding on acrylics to make it possible. His knuckles hardening as harshly as his back, expelling his sweatshirt for the body's becoming. His ears likewise stretched as his nails— and then not. Surely, Two wasn't bearing witness to this level of metamorphosis— surely, they mind was playing that game it had been playing as of late— seeing and hearing what couldn't be mutually seen and heard. It was the mind making Two more and more alone, but for all that factual argument, Two was positive an armadillo was rolling them a blunt. He winked at Two— *you're not alone in this. I can't stay human all the time, too.*

It's possible Two transformed Saint into an armadillo to make his being a man more tolerable. It also didn't feel like much of a conscious decision, this shift from one animal into another. It was the same sensation Two had when they offered Saint to come inside their water-logged home— that they had known him, known him lifetimes over. Some Octavia Butler shit, Two categorized it as. Two hoped it was a case of overactive imagination but wasn't ready to delude theyself. They couldn't unsee what was happening in front of them, another dimension of the first time Two saw their mother naked, seeing where the doctors cut them out, seeing the hair and overt claim on womanhood, the wrinkles and taut skin both. Saint was exposed somehow, had revealed himself to Two, knowingly or otherwise. This gesture, if nothing before, made him family to Two. It would be hard from this moment to write this evening off as random, as *yea, so cooky, just let the Landshark delivery dude inside,* there was a resonance, a pulse back and forth in time, connecting Two and Saint to the earth they stood on, to, inexplicably, each other.

And it's equally possible that this is the feeling most black femmes or women feel toward black men or masc folks. This insatiable connection, desperate need to be close, to protect, to guard them from the rest of the world, knowing the rest of the world is in the thick of hunting season, hunting exactly for them.

When is it not war? Two worried if it was a perpetual war, one that would take every generation of humanity and even after that to upend, would Two ever be able to ask of theyself to not make space for men? If it's war, they need shelter— how can you deny shelter to a solider? But the solider in question never recognizes their war— the other side of the trench, the other fighting in uniform.

But even this silent physical shift in Saint was less jarring than a few nights back, around when Two's mind began to turn, when that white dude climbed into their bed, shoes off, feet making chaos of their air, and climbed further, all up on Two, wanting, hungry. Two's body fell to a hush prehistoric— the chill through them akin to a cold front, all warmth lost from their world. The white man still intent on getting what they thought was theirs, writhing and kissing on them. Like the perpetual trauma response, Two in that moment began asking theyself the questions, *did I ask for this? Do I want this? My body is gone somehow, I don't want to be inside of it anymore. Is it me or is it him? What is the contagion? Will he leave if I just let him have me? Will he stay in my house all night, whether I give myself up or not? Is this his house now? Was it ever my house? Where do I live? How can I say it? How can I ask him to leave?*

We were hanging out— was I flirting? Was the flirting suggesting a physical response? What has this been all this time— getting fast food dinners, texting, watching a movie here and there— was it all leading up to this moment? If so, then why can't I move? Why can't I breathe? Why do I feel like I am being taken from me? How much farther am I going to let this go? Is it even up to me anymore? Is this like the power of attorney, where someone sees I can't fend for myself so they take up that function on my behalf? If I say no now, will he hate me? Do I care if he hates me? Do I hate me and that's how I got here? Is it like a vampire where if I invite him in my home, whatever happens to me is my fault? I did want sex, but did I want it now, with this person, in this place, at this time? Am I nothing? Maybe I have always been nothing and this is what happens to nothing— nothing. This is nothing. Right? This is a non-event, I'm sure this happens all the time, this isn't even a this this is just an event, like brushing my teeth, it will be over soon, unless it won't, unless it lasts all night and in the morning, will he want to eat with me after, when is after, get off me get off me get off—

And he did, confused, staring at Two. Embarrassed. Pink with lust and pink with anger. Two had replayed that night on repeat in their mind since it happened, began developing a ritual to repurpose their body, make it feel again. And of course the white man did hate them, or decided Two would make misery of their miserable choices, and soon got as far away from Two as a human could be, and fine. Fine. Two decided it wasn't groundbreaking, men taking and non-men not knowing how to extricate themselves. It wasn't groundbreaking, wasn't interesting, wasn't new, so Two decided it could be forgotten. But Two's body couldn't forget. It would shake within itself, it would cramp and clot. Any motivation left it the moment Two required movement, any desire for who Two actually wanted to touch and be touched by retired, vacating the system. Two was numb, and in this walking paralysis, created a shift not unlike Saint's. Two's blonde hairs on they stomach harvesting into a pelt of stark white. They moles, black and brown becoming freckles and everywhere, large as they ears. They hands, hooves now. They feet, hooves now. They ears, more outward and outward, small tents pitched on either side of they head. They nose— a hue, black, button and tender. Eyes already so brown they were black, something Two heard most days in elementary school, around the time Kenny suggested Two wanted to be a slave because they cried during the educational video about the slave girl that learned to write her name in the dirt with a stick. It didn't take much for Two to become a deer in their own bed. They wondered if they practiced now on the porch with Saint if Saint would mind, would freak out and bolt, would notice at all because what if this is entirely in they head?

An armadillo and a deer shared a blunt on the porch littered with cigarette butts, beer cans, magnolias. In their states as animals, they could shake their histories as humans— the mental hospitals, the beaches in Ghana, the white men in their beds, the football coaches' callous direction, the 40 acres, their black, the ships it incepted from, their loneliness, a trait honed by humanity and reviled. As animals, they could be instinct and survival. The notion to thrive was eradicated. There was a sense of being, of sitting inside oneself and enjoying the residence. Two knew they couldn't maintain this form forever, that in another glitch, they would return back into the bodies they were birthed as, but for as long as they could stand it, could they be these figments? These creatures Two saw on a daily basis, curling up and rolling across the highway? Standing in headlights like a fool to their doom? Two already felt as though they had been headlight stared down and lost. Saint had what most armadillos have— a defense mechanism that doesn't suit the 21st century world we reside in. When an armadillo is confronted by a predator, before they roll up and away, they leap, approximately 4 feet into the air. Why? Who the fuck knows. But adapting to the current world has proved a farce, given that cars are about that high off the ground, leaving the armadillo to get hit with such accuracy, that so many of them are dead before they have the chance to live. To be a black man and to be an armadillo, then, were not so different. To be a black femme and a deer— mutual experience.

Saint passes Two the blunt, their bodies reverted back to humanity for a shudder. The ritual commences— weed, air, inhale, exhale, repeat. Every few exchanges, Two sees them for their animal counterparts, then not, until the blunt is completed. They don't talk anymore. There's really not much more to say. Their loneliness is matched with drugs, alleviated for a moment out of them. The smoke a catalyst for alchemy. A nihilism reflected and held. Communion.

Two got up and started walking. Saint followed in suit. Glitch— a deer and armadillo start walking. Following in suit. Glitch— a deer and armadillo are on a boat, sailing for the Americas from Ghana. Glitch— two black bodies on a boat in the same direction. Glitch— two black bodies on a plantation in Mississippi. Glitch— an armadillo and a deer, grazing in Mississippi. Glitch— two black bodies are trees and are on the trees. Glitch— two black bodies share a blunt. Glitch— one black body is in the house, the other on the football field. Glitch— one black body is in the house, the other on the cotton field. Glitch— the water doesn't agree with you. Glitch— there is no you, just the 5 women in your head and the scars on your back. Glitch— a deer orders sushi on a rainy night. Glitch— an armadillo gets side-eyed by white police in Dodge Challengers. Glitch— a deer walks into a bar with a white woman. Glitch— a black man walks into a bar with a white woman. Glitch— a black boy whistles. Glitch— a white woman lies. Glitch — a man is a man and all his stories at a woman, femme. Glitch— a mother tells you how to hold a man's stories. Glitch— a man brands a woman and she is chattel. Glitch— a man hunts a woman down and she is a deer. Glitch— a name reverberates three continents and lands growing a nation of itself. Glitch— a culture is sucked dry. Glitch— a deer and an armadillo walk into a bar. Glitch— a man wants a woman to become all the women he's loved before you. Glitch— a deer loves a woman and is a woman and isn't a woman at all. Glitch— a man doesn't care. Glitch— who owns you now?

Two and Saint reached highway 7 and stood on the right side of it. Time to cross, to get to the strip mall with the best taco shop in the town. The sushi left discarded, a beginning gone to rot. They wait for the right breath, like double dutch, an opening.

Two raced out first. It's up for debate whether they saw the semi or not, whether it was a false double dutch move or a more formal attempt at leaving they body and the world. Saint charged in front of Two. A deer and an armadillo in headlights. A crash. Two bodies on highway 7, stunted and ready to become dirt. A freedom. Only each body aware that they would do this again. Every glitch an energy, neither created or destroyed. They'd see each other on the flip side. Likely tomorrow. Likely prey, again. What their traumas made and unmade of them. On the side of the highway, the wheat coming into bloom. A blonde field.

Aziza Barnes is blk & alive. Aziza's first collection, *i be but i ain't*, was the 2015 winner of the Pament River Prize from YesYes Books. Barnes' play, *BLKS*, was produced in Chicago at the Steppenwolf Theater in 2017, and is to be produced at Wooly Mammoth Theater in DC and MCC Theater in New York in 2019. Barnes' is a cohost of the podcast, *The Poetry Gods* and is a Cave Canem fellow.

For events and catalog information:
notacult.media

Not a Cult's Fall 2019 catalog

Hermosa by Yesika Salgado
ISBN 978-1-945649-33-2

the blind pig by Aziza Barnes
ISBN 978-1-945649-32-5

From Rufio to Zuko by Dante Basco
Lost Boys Edition ISBN 978-1-945649-35-6
Fire Nation Edition ISBN 978-1-945649-36-3

Books distributed by SCB Distributors